COW PIES

A messy journey through
the pasture of life

The outlandish musings of
Gene McDougall and Nelson Campbell

AuthorHouse™
1663 Liberty Drive
Bloomington, IN 47403
www.authorhouse.com
Phone: 1-800-839-8640

© 2011 by Gene McDougall & Nelson Campbell. All rights reserved.

No part of this book may be reproduced, stored in a retrieval system, or transmitted by any means without the written permission of the author.

First published by AuthorHouse   09/13/2011

ISBN: 978-1-4634-6000-6 (sc)
ISBN: 978-1-4634-5999-4 (ebk)

Library of Congress Control Number: 2011914581

Printed in the United States of America

Any people depicted in stock imagery provided by Thinkstock are models, and such images are being used for illustrative purposes only.
Certain stock imagery © Thinkstock.

This book is printed on acid-free paper.

Because of the dynamic nature of the Internet, any web addresses or links contained in this book may have changed since publication and may no longer be valid. The views expressed in this work are solely those of the author and do not necessarily reflect the views of the publisher, and the publisher hereby disclaims any responsibility for them.

Published by:
Author House

Gene McDougall
2811 E. Bel Aire Drive
Arlington Heights IL
60004-6605 USA

Nelson Campbell
500 Thames Parkway
Park Ridge, IL
60068-3690 USA

Copyright © 2000
by Gene McDougall and Nelson Campbell
Original edition, first printing

Second printing: 2011
Printed in the United States of America

FOREWORD

"Colors fade, temples crumble, empires fall, but wise words endure" - Edward Thorndike.

(Editor's note: To be fair, it must be said that Thorndike was probably not describing this specific book, since it had not yet been written at the time of his death in 1949. Things don't always work out.)

DISCLAIMER

While we all have a right to express our opinions about people in the public eye, private people are afforded more protection under the law. So we have changed or omitted the names of all the louts and buffoons we've met during our precarious journey through the minefield of life. In some cases, the people we've described are composites of assorted jerks we have known. Except for public figures, any similarity to any real person living or dead is purely coincidental. The authors' perceptions and opinions are just that – perceptions and opinions - nothing more.

TABLE OF CONTENTS

Chapter 1   1988 & 1989   1
Temperance, tennis, ladies of the evening, televangelists, Guam and the South Korean Olympic Games.

Chapter 2   1990 & 1991   23
Sun City West, Warsaw (Indiana), journalism, sex, Guam and arcane references to the Clarence Thomas confirmation hearings.

Chapter 3   1992 & 1993   43
Tennis, mail fraud, high school reunions, the S&L scandal, investing, cults, Waco, Minnesota and a pitiful cry for help from Hortense Snavely.

Chapter 4   1994 & 1995   75
Tennis, Santa Claus, voice mail, grammar, a satanic cult and a trip to London.

Chapter 5   1996   99
Grammar, the homeless, publishing, tennis, sophistry and writing.

Chapter 6   1997   129
Moldova, grammar, sex and some interesting get-rich-quick schemes.

Chapter 7   1998   147
Hypocrites, voice mail, tennis, sex and plagiarism. Names are named.

Chapter 8   1999   185
More names are named, causing one of the writers to go undercover.

Chapter 1
1988 & 1989

Temperance, tennis, ladies of the evening, televangelists, Guam, and the South Korean Olympic Games.

Reverend Jones' legendary assistant, Clyde Lindstrom

Reverend Elton Jones
Rescue Mission, Redneck, Texas

January 12, 1988

To: Reverend Clarence Klotz

Dear Brother,

Perhaps you have heard of my nationwide temperance campaign. Each year for the past decade, I have made a tour of Texas, Florida, and southern Georgia, up through Indiana, Iowa and Illinois – delivering sermons on the evils of drinking. I have been accompanied on this tour by my young friend and assistant, Clyde Lindstrom. Clyde, a man of good family and excellent background, is a pathetic example of a life ruined by excessive indulgence in whiskey and women.

Clyde has always appeared with me at my lectures - sitting on the platform wheezing and staring at the audience through bleary, bloodshot eyes, sweating profusely, picking his nose, wetting his pants, passing gas and making obscene gestures while I pointed him out as an example of what overindulgence can do to a person.

Last fall Clyde died. A mutual friend, Gene McDougall, has given me your name and I wonder if you would be available to take Clyde's place on this year's spring tour.

Yours in faith,

Elton

Clarence Klotz
Sheffield Island Lighthouse off Norwalk, Connecticut

January 22, 1988

Dear Rev. Jones,

Out here on the stern and rockbound New England coast, where one develops an intoxicating kinship with the relentless, eternal sea, I am seriously weighing your kind invitation to join your crusade against the evils of drink.

I, too, am waging such a campaign. My current flock are some of life's loneliest men, the lighthouse keepers. Usually single and separated from the carefree, gregarious, more advantaged mainland life, they fall victim to John Barleycorn. Loneliness may make a philosopher and creative genius of a Thoreau, but how many Thoreaus are among the plodding workmen who keep the harbor lights burning and the channel gongs sounding?

Is not the lighthouse keeper like so many other forgotten men: the night watchman, the rural postman, the street cleaner, the steamship oiler, the elevator operator, the garbage collector? What of those whose dreams have been shattered once too often, brother? What can we say to those whose lives are on the back side of the hill? How can we save those who have turned to drink as a last resort? The lighthouseman sees gay yachtsmen at play, but he cannot participate. He sees the glorious sun rise out of the waters, but his memories may be warped by visions of the Titanic, the Andria Doria, the Morro Castle, the Lusitania or the Lady Elgin. Some were in his territory, some were not, but he knows that all might have been. As he looks over the white caps at dusk, he may be haunted by these immortal lines from "Lost on the Lady Elgin":

There were husbands and wives...
Little children lost their lives;
It was sad when that good ship went down.

It's sad when any ship goes down, brother. Your charges and mine are ships, and it's our task to see that they don't go down in a lightning-fast world where temptations abound. This philosophy has sustained me in my work over the years among sheepherders in the Colorado valleys, down-and-outers in the hobo jungles of Nashville, elderly widows in the antebellum mansions of Charleston and unemployed fishermen along the Big Bend of the Columbia River. Again, your mission could be my next calling. How soon must you have my decision? I can be reached at the Retired Seamen's Home, Box 93, Southport, Conn. 06430. In the meantime, my sympathies to Clyde's family.

Affectionately,

The Venerable Reverend Elton Jones

Ilikai Hotel, Honolulu, HI

February 10, 1988

Clarence Klotz
Sheffield Island Lighthouse

Dear Brother,

A simple yes or no would have been sufficient. Unfortunately, by the time your reply reached me, I had already started my spring tour. In fact, I am writing this from Hawaii, which is this year's first stop.

What I am trying to say is that you have, so to speak, "missed the boat." I do, however, feel that you are the best possible replacement for poor Clyde, and remain hopeful that you will be able to join the tour next year.

Sanguinely,

Elton

Clarence Klotz
Old Potomac Settlement House
Washington, D. C.

February 21, 1988

Brother Elton,

Aye, lad, you were always the brash one. Quick to decision and uncompromising to pragmatism and the deft nuances of life.

It's well and good that you're on your spring tour, but life cannot be so conveniently compartmented, brother. Problems cannot await the start of an invocation nor do they end with a benediction. As I am called to serve alcoholics in the settlement houses in the shadows of our nation's Capitol, geisha girls in Tokyo, sheepherders in the Rockies, unemployed roughnecks in the oil fields and aged members of the Society of Quilters, Needlepointers and Tatters (SQUINT) in the Old South - so I may walk into your tour one day.

I'll be unannounced, but I'll have a message, and I trust you'll find a place for me.

Ethereally but pragmatically,

Clarence

Reverend Elton Jones

April 15, 1988

Dear Clarence,

Word has leaked out to my flock that we have a tentative agreement to work together on my tour next year. I don't want to take advantage of our newly formed relationship, but since you are known to be a major investor in the Hackers Haven Tennis Club, I have been urged by my friends to ask you to use your influence to get the following improvements made in their tennis program:

1. Add surf & turf to the lunch league menu.

2. Have an annual Slow Serve tournament.

3. Hold a Heart Bypass tournament with a huge cash prize for the winner.

4. Sacrifice a virgin, should one be found among your membership.

Although my experience and expertise do not extend to tennis or business, these suggestions seem reasonable to me so I am passing them on to you in the spirit of enlightened progress for the benefit of all. Perhaps we do not have to wait for next year's tour to begin working together to make this a better world. I hope you share the joy and excitement I feel at this moment!

Magnanimously,

Elton

Clarence Klotz
Somewhere on the range of life

May 15, 1988

Dear Brother Elton,

I appreciate your worldly concerns as expressed in your recent letter, but as the shadows lengthen, I feel compelled to devote my waking hours to higher causes. There is dignity in any labor and a sense of contribution in any cause, but do understand that I must now regard myself as a citizen of the world, not a mere cog in a local enterprise.

However, your four points are well taken. Permit me to address them in order:

1. Management has been under the impression that tuna salad and ham sandwiches qualified as "surf and turf." Rest assured that a lobster-and-steak fare will be introduced immediately.

2. Management has hesitated to conduct a Slow Serve event because the winner would be a foregone conclusion, thus interest would be minimal. A variation, however, is under consideration, and now that you are a net-rushing monster you may be intrigued. It's a Beat Your Serve to the Net competition, with all winners receiving a lollipop of his or her choice.

3. We'll agree to the heart bypass tournament, the promise of a "huge cash prize" being the only issue.

4. Your request that we sacrifice a virgin is academic since official club records show no virgins over 13 on the rolls.

But back to deeper concerns. Ere we meet again, I shall have ministered to gauchos in Patagonia, Eskimos in the Yukon, Berbers in the Sahara and ladies of the evening on the streets of Los Angeles. Keep the faith.

Ethereally,

Clarence

Pre-sacrifice blessing

Reverend Elton Jones

May 20, 1988

Dear Clarence,

I have struggled mightily with the news contained in your last missive. While I applaud your mission to save the gauchos of Patagonia, Eskimos in the Yukon and Berbers in the Sahara, I have anguished over your avowed intention to minister to the ladies of the evening on the streets of Los Angeles. Ever since the demise of my fast friends and brothers of the cloth, the good Reverends Swaggart and Bakker, the Los Angeles ladies of the evening have been my province exclusively. It would be a needless – and, in fact, wasteful – duplication of effort if you and I were to both spend our time and resources helping the same group of unfortunates.

While on the subject of resources, I am sure you know how expensive Los Angeles is. In order to continue my work there, a constant inflow of funds is required, and my ministry is facing a financial crisis at the present time. I call upon you to open your heart and pockets to save me so that I might save others. I have enclosed a letter I received just today from our mutual friend, Gene McDougall, to show you what generosity still exists in this world, with the hope that you will follow his inspirational example.

Desperately,

Elton

Gene McDougall
born again sinner

May 20, 1988

Dear Reverend Jones,

Please accept the enclosed check to use in your wonderful work. You will notice that it is quite large. That is because it is my entire life savings. I am ashamed to say that before I saw the light I had earmarked this money to provide food, shelter, clothing and medical supplies and services for my wife and me in our retirement – but now I know I can free myself of such selfish concerns by turning the money over to you in the certain knowledge that the Lord will provide.

I feel better already!

Joyously,

Gene

Clarence Klotz
Tent City, Washington, D. C.

June 27, 1988

Dear Elton,

Word of your earth-shaking victories over Paul French and Irv Converse has reached the halls of government. Our elected representatives, many in severe shock, seek explanations. So does this old campaigner, who twice defeated Converse in the 60s but lost to him in the Western semifinals in '81.*

There may be a congressional inquiry. How, they're asking from coast to coast, can a cantankerous old reprobate be 25 per cent improved just two years after a quintuple bypass? What's involved? Steroids? Blood doping? Astrology? UFOs? Communism?

So there'll be no spiritualizing tonight. Better we spend our time in learning if there's something new in your drinking water, whether you have taken up transcendental meditation, whether your surgeon transplanted some genes (no pun intended) or whether you've imported a youth-reclaiming potion from the Amazon jungles.

In any event, congratulations, but stand by. You may be called to testify. Meanwhile, try to remain your humble, lovable self.

Incredulously,

Clarence

*For which he earned $25, thus becoming an official "pro" and forever contaminating himself. Should this figure not impress you, remember it hasn't been adjusted for inflation.

Reverend Elton Jones

July 15, 1988

Dear Clarence,

Thank you for your recent paean regarding my tennis rebirth. Ironically, I have been learning of the Clarence Klotz legend in bits and pieces over the years. As a result, I have become obsessed with the admittedly grandiose notion that one day I could actually step onto the court with this man who, among his other accomplishments, is said to have once been the number one player in the 45-year-old bracket of the Chicago District Tennis Association.

I realize this is only a dream at this point, with hard questions to face and obstacles to overcome. For instance, would the two of us ever be in the Chicago area at the same time? Even if this were to happen, would a pro deign to play an amateur? Am I being too presumptuous? These and other questions prey upon me.

Please advise, keeping in mind that I am a sensitive, fragile person and do not react well to rejection.

Gingerly,

Elton

Clarence Klotz

August 5, 1988

Dear Brother,

Word of your clutch managerial efforts, the brand of savvy that enables tennis players down 1-5, 15-40, to win sets, has reached me on my newest pilgrimage.

Would that this magic be applied to the spiritual challenges confronting you.

Are your motivational techniques sufficiently concrete that they might be codified in book form? If so, please consider me as a possible agent. The pickings are slim in the tent cities of the land.

The previously mentioned congressional investigations are off. Your 3.5 team's incredible comeback in the Chicago-area playoffs has upstaged your victories over Converse and French, leaving House and Senate members to wonder if even more wondrous wonders might lie ahead. Who wants to be investigating Mt. St. Helens while all California is dropping into the Pacific Ocean?

Keep the faith,

Clarence

Clarence Klotz

December 18, 1988

Dear Brother,

I'm just passing through your area and won't have time to break bread. Thus via a typewriter at my Chicago mission I'll wish you a Merry Christmas and your ever inspirational work continued success. There's just time enough before I catch the westbound Greyhound. My destination this time is your old stomping grounds, Guam. There I'll be ministering to Chimorro outriggermen and others beyond The Big Reef.

These are men outside life's mainstream, hence so deserving of our attention. What matter class or station when the human spirit is at stake? Is not water but a continuation of the land just as death is but a continuation of life? Is not the Almighty on the sea just the same as on the land? Who has lived who has not ventured beyond The Big Reef? Who can justifiably mouth platitudes about life who has never seen life? Does a man qualify for sainthood if he has never known temptation? And what is peace? Is there peace simply because no shots were fired between newscasts or when we can't hear the cries of the victims?

Because of the language barrier out there, I'll be taking a course in Basic Pidgin English before I start circuit-riding. How I wish an old Pacific hand like you were with me - a man who knows the people and bears such a vital message. But you have your flocks, and I have mine. Remember that no man is an island. All that we take out of the lives of others comes back into our own. After January 10, I'll be at the Blue Pacific Inn just outside Agana. Pray for me, and may destiny speed the day when we can resume our philosophical discussions.

Doing God's work,

Clarence

Reverend Elton Jones

December 25, 1988

Dear Clarence,

Learning that you intend to spread the word on Guam has caused my blood to run cold! I cannot believe that you fully grasp the folly of your decision. Before it is too late, let me give you some insight into the true nature of this godforsaken place.

Strange rites are practiced there, and, in fact, I know of at least one marine who was practicing animal husbandry until they caught him at it one day. Bad enough that he was dating outside his species, but he had chosen what most of us felt was one of the least attractive water buffaloes on the island.

Trust me – my military service on Guam from 1949 to 1952 still haunts me. Do NOT go there. Your work is important, but there are other places in need of your services. Have you considered Calcutta or Bangladesh?

Indulgently,

Elton

Clarence Klotz
Old Rockbridge Inn
Cornwall, Connecticut

March 30, 1989

Dear Brother Elton,

As the ice starts breaking and the Berkshires show their first signs of spring. I'm journeying the back trails of New England, working with those struggling representatives of old-time free enterprise, the Yankee general store owners. O, that you could be with me.

No one has carried the torch for business more than the Yankee merchant. Yet no entrepreneur is in sadder shape in this era of bigness than the small store proprietor...the small grocer, the small hardwareman, the small haberdasher.

Let the politicians say how much of the free enterprise system is at stake when the small businessmen go bankrupt in droves. Let the economists say whether relief is obtainable through diversification or specialized marketing. Let the sociologists say whether we should care if the neighborhood deli must stay open 16 hours a day to compete with the supermarket in the new shopping center. Let the lawyers decide when the buying squeeze becomes "in restraint of trade" rather than simply "tough competition."

My job, brother, is with the seemingly powerless victims, many of who are fifth and sixth generation proprietors with family trees going back to Bunker Hill and Concord Bridge.

Things aren't what they used to be in picturesque New England. Things are great in metropolitan Boston but not so in the countryside. O, it's great for tourists...the Revolutionary War buffs, the musket collectors, the skiers, the antique fanciers, the New Yorkers who want to escape the summer heat, the midwesterners who want to see the ultimate in fall colors and the outlanders who want to hear people talk like Ajax Cassidy or the buggy driver in the Pepperidge Farm commercial. But how about the folks who have to live there 365 days a year and eke out a living by selling to each other? What is life like when the last gawking tourist has gone and realities set in? Is it not easy, brother, to liken the Yankee storekeeper to the ploughman in Gray's "Elegy"?

> The curfew tolls the knell of parting day,
> The lowing herd winds slowly o'er the lea,
> The ploughman homeward plods his weary way
> And leaves the world to darkness and to me.

There's nothing like a peaceful crossroads in colonial Connecticut to remind us of the soul's eternal quest for peace and tranquility. How I wish you were on this mission with me! Your stirring message would add so much. Tonight I'm hosting my first group in this area - at the Old Rockbridge Inn on the Old Cornwall Turnpike, hard by Red Mountain. You can reach me there.

Warmest regards,

Clarence

Reverend Elton Jones

April 19, 1989

Dear Clarence,

It was good to hear from you, and uplifting indeed to learn of your noble efforts on behalf of the backwoods unfortunates in New England. However, I'll come right to the point – I have discovered a higher calling.

What are the most helpless of earth's creatures? Surely not man, who has ostensibly been given the gift of reason. No, it is the animals that have no control over their own destiny. They have been, and continue to be, victimized by man.

I call your attention to the recent Olympic Games in South Korea. To most people, the news that water polo had been introduced as a sanctioned event was of no concern, but to those of us who care about horses, this was a tragic development.

Can I count on your support in my campaign to have water polo banned from future Olympic Games?

Sanguinely,

Elton

Clarence Klotz

October 3, 1989

My dear Elton,

So sorry to miss you. I was in the Chicago area briefly for the purpose of conducting interviews on an exciting new ministry. As cool nights and shedding trees warn that winter is nigh, it seemed an ideal time to complete arrangements for upcoming work among Eskimos, Laplanders, Greenlanders and residents along the Minnesota-Ontario border.

You seemed so perfect for this charge. Don't despair at the failed connection. There will be other opportunities to serve.

Relentlessly,

Clarence

Clarence Klotz

December, 1989

Dear Colleague Elton,

Tonight I'm in the Rockies where majestic peaks encourage meditation among even the rankest unbelievers and one can re-assess a misspent life.

I'm working with men and women from various chapters of Gamblers Anonymous, people who have forfeited what might have been productive lives at the $2 windows of temptation.

When will we learn God's Odds, brother? When will we learn that money isn't even in the first 10 of life's satisfactions? And isn't life itself a gamble, a precious commodity that passes only once, whose pitfalls could never be completely insured against, even by King Midas?

I wish you could attend some of our sessions here. What glorious reward there is in seeing just one gambler in 50 see the light, repent and return whole to his once productive walk of life. We hope to prevail on Pete Rose to chair an upcoming seminar, and we eagerly seek your input.

Affectionately,

Clarence

Chapter 2
1990 & 1991

Sun City West, Warsaw (Indiana), journalism, sex, Guam
and arcane references to the Clarence Thomas confirmation hearings.

Are you kidding? Clarence Thomas on the Supreme Court?

Reverend Elton Jones

January 15, 1990

Dear Brother Clarence,

You and others of the faith have ministered to a diverse assortment of unfortunates including gauchos in Patagonia, Eskimos in the Yukon, Berbers in the Sahara, ladies of the evening in Los Angeles, the lost souls on Guam and even gamblers in the Rockies. But who has shown concern for the most maligned of all – the snowbirds of Phoenix? No one - until now.

I have accepted the challenge. Yes, I am now in Arizona, and for the next several months I will live among these people as one of them, adopting their lifestyle and spending day after pointless day doing nothing more than swimming, sunbathing and playing tennis – the better to understand these pathetic, unproductive creatures. Do not grieve for me, for I make this sacrifice willingly, secure in the knowledge that I will be a better man for it.

Notwithstanding my earlier remarks, all is not gloom and sorrow here. A higher wisdom has provided a certain balance by putting people together, some of whom repeat themselves, while others are unable to remember what they just heard. Can anyone doubt that there is indeed a great plan?

Your assistance is always highly valued, so if you are out this way during the winter and wish to volunteer your services, my temporary headquarters will be in Sun City West, Arizona. I'm in the book.

Stoically,

Elton

Clarence Klotz
Youth Hostel, Champaign, IL

March 16, 1990

Dear Brother Elton,

O, that we could walk again together across the tree-lined quadrangles of academe. What joys be the ivory towers of innocence and idealism, the safe harbors from which you and I launched our crusades into the infernos of life.

I am in this college community for a fortnight, working with groups of 60 and 70-year-old graduate students, men who have never found themselves and seek paths to fulfillment before it is too late. I need assistance and fondly hope you might temporarily forsake your quest for the national 60-and-over tennis championships and catch an IC for Champaign.

As a fellow seeker of truth, unmindful of barbs from the unthinking crowd, I know you'll empathize with me. Who can better understand an old war horse of the missionary trail than a contemporary of similar calling? Virtue is its own reward, brother. How could we ever put a price tag on the satisfaction that comes from doing a good deed, or saving a soul, or steering a fellow human being toward long-elusive fulfillment? Do not the immortal words of Scott apply...

> Sound, sound the clarion, fill the fife;
> To all the sensual world proclaim:
> One crowded hour of glorious life
> Is worth an age without a name.

Do call me at the Hostel, brother, and let me know of your work.

Anxiously,

Clarence

Reverend Elton Jones

July 13, 1990

Dear Brother Clarence,

Greetings from historic Warsaw. Now that the iron curtain is no more, I had to see for myself what several decades of Communist rule have done to this city.

To begin with, it is a much smaller place than I had expected. On the other hand, it came as no surprise that the living standards are primitive indeed in comparison to our own. Yet the inhabitants are cheerful and friendly - and almost to a man they are able to converse in English as long as the conversation is kept simple - "Where is the toilet? - I am hungry. - Where are the girls?"

Of course, modern technology is not part of everyday life in this part of the world. For instance, hard-surface tennis courts have not yet been introduced to the area, so they are forced to play on gravel. Having known nothing better, they seem content with their lot.

In light of all I have learned here, it seems to me that my services could be of more value elsewhere. Therefore, ever in search of more meaningful work, I will be wending my way westward within the next few days.

Our paths are sure to cross sometime in the not too distant future as we traverse the globe spreading the word. I revel in the certain knowledge that this grand day draws ever closer even as I type these words.

Joyously,

Elton

(EDITOR'S NOTE: POSTMARKED WARSAW, INDIANA)

Clarence Klotz
Youth Hostel
Somewhere on the Mississippi

August 3, 1990

Dear Brother Elton,

The last time I saw Warsaw (how would that be for a song title?) it was a little different from what you describe. Can we be talking about the same city?

To each his own vantage point, brother. What matter the terrain if heart and soul are on the same frequency? Everyone at the senior citizens' home delights in your tennis successes. Alas, this old circuit rider knows little of manly sports. Who was it who said grass is for cows, asphalt is for cars and clay is for tennis?

This summer I'm working with old showboat sailors on the Mississippi, trying to give them new life and confidence as they pursue what seems to the madding crowd an anachronistic calling. I know your thoughts are with me.

Remember that the past is but prologue, that the future is now and that tomorrow is the first day of the rest of our lives.

Affectionately,

Clarence

Elton Jones Rescue Mission
Florida Chapter

December 3, 1990

Dear Clarence,

Although it may seem that my coming here to Florida is nothing more than a way to escape the harsh, cold winter of the north, nothing could be farther from the truth. I am here to minister to my flock, which is the only reason I ever travel.

Having said that, I hasten to assure you that this trip will not be without its pleasant moments. As luck would have it, our mutual friend, Gene McDougall, will be participating in tennis and table tennis at the Florida State Senior Olympics while I am here, so I will be found among the fans as they gather to watch the action. I also understand that he will be in Arizona for that state's Senior Olympics in February. It strikes me that here is a man who actually seems to go out of his way to avoid any involvement in productive or worthwhile endeavors of any sort.

Let us be at peace knowing that he and those of his ilk are sure to find the true way in their own good time.

Serenely,

Elton

Elton Jones Rescue Mission

May 10, 1991

Dear Clarence,

Egad, what jolting news! I have just learned that our friend Gene McDougall, inspired by your notable success in the field of journalism, has dedicated his life to following in your footsteps. Having neither the talent to write a book nor the courage to use his own name, he has been writing a blasphemous, mean-spirited, column (as Uncle Randy, advisor to the wretched) for the local chapter of a prestigious international organization. The fact that his work has actually been published is a triumph of desire over all that is logical and right in the universe, yet it is a fact.

These are strange and confusing times, with many of us reaching deep inside ourselves to find what is right and what is not – and not always knowing when and if we have found the answer, or whether there is an answer to find. As brothers of the cloth, I feel I can confide to you that sometimes I grow weary, and have even considered giving up the good fight. Only the realization that people such as you and me are all that stand between the Gene McDougalls of the world and their eternal damnation gives me the strength to carry on.

God help me,

Elton

Uncle Randy
advisor to the wretched

May 12, 1991

Dear Clarence,

I enjoyed your call the other day. You mentioned that you felt ill-equipped to handle a problem recently presented to you by one of your flock, and asked if I would help, since you felt that my advice column is the best of its genre. How can I say no?

As I understand it, the subject is a 78-year-old widow who remarried one year ago. Her new husband beats her and has spent her entire inheritance of $200,000 on other women. Since they are now penniless, her husband wants her to go to work, but she has no business skills.

Your responsibility is clear. Tell her that she must first get rid of her negative attitude. Nobody likes a whiner. There are plenty of careers out there that do not require formal training. Investment counseling, politics and prostitution are a few that readily come to mind.

I hope this advice will help turn her life around.

Glad to help,

Uncle Randy

Shady Lane Home for the Baffled

May 14, 1991

Dear Uncle Randy,

My husband went out for a newspaper and a cup of coffee in June, 1949, and hasn't returned. I am starting to get worried.

Should I be so untrusting? Or should I simply get on with my life? I will be 94 in August. Or maybe it's September.

I have little formal training but am uplifted by your report of opportunities in the fields of investment counseling, prostitution and politics.

Thank you for being so sensitive. My good friend, Clarence Klotz, told me you could help.

Devoted

Uncle Randy
advisor to the wretched

May 17, 1991

Dear Devoted,

You did the right thing in coming to me for help. No, it would not be untrusting of you to get on with your life and pursue a career in politics, prostitution or investment counseling. After all, you would still have the option of resuming your married life when your husband returns.

I believe the most lucrative of the three fields could be politics if you do it right. To get pointers on how best to manipulate the system to your own personal advantage, contact Congressman Dan Rostenkowski. Here is a man who, while becoming wealthy at the expense of the taxpayers, has dedicated himself to raising the taxes of the elderly and cutting back the government benefits they paid for throughout their working lives. And he keeps getting re-elected. Is this one slick dude or what?

Of course, if your conscience prevents you from going into politics or investment counseling, the only remaining viable alternative is prostitution. At your age, the most obvious advantage of this choice is that it would keep you off your feet.

Whatever your choice, please accept my sincere best wishes for happiness and success. The bill for my services ($100) is being sent to you under separate cover.

Cordially,

Uncle Randy

Clarence Klotz
FISHIN' MISSION
Lake in the Clouds
Baffin Island

May 28, 1991

Dear Uncle Randy,

I'll be far from the madding crowd during early summer, working with a group of "old codgers," those legendary lost souls whose livelihoods have come to depend on a modicum of deception. Who, as the shadows lengthen, can look in the mirror day after day under such circumstances?

Meanwhile, please do not think ill of me if you are sued for damages in the wake of your recent counsel. The net result of three readings was two bruised ribs from laughing and a shoulder injury when I fell off the chair. Given our litigious society and the outrageous nature of your advice, I feel certain you are used to this.

Affectionately,

Clarence

Clarence Klotz
in transit

June 25, 1991

Dear Brother Elton,

I've departed my assignment with "old codgers" at the Fishin' Mission with a feeling of great satisfaction. People <u>are</u> reclaimable, friend.

I'm now on my way to the foothills of the Ozarks where I'll hold sessions at the National Association of Mom and Pop Store Owners (NAMAPSO), persons whom life seems to be passing by. Perhaps we're all in the same boat, and it's up to you and me to find antidotes.

Wish me well. Until my next communiqué I'll be a knight of the road, unreachable.

Devotedly,

Clarence

Reverend Elton Jones

August 8, 1991

Dear Clarence,

I was thrilled to hear that you plan to spend some time in the foothills of the Ozarks, since I have a friend who is a native of those parts. He is an interesting chap – about our age and never married, although he tells me that many years ago a friend offered him the hand of his virgin 15-year-old daughter. He turned down the offer because he felt that "if she warn't good enough for her own kin, she warn't good enough for me".

Well, how embarrassing. I seem to be dwelling upon sex. I think my obsession with the subject stems from my having had to wait so long for my first time. Since I was ninth in line, I had to wait about an hour.

Forgive me for rambling on so shamelessly, but as a brother of the cloth, I know you realize confession is good for the soul – and who, if not you, could I count upon to be compassionate and non-judgmental as he reads these words?

I feel cleansed.

Gratefully,

Gene

Guam Lobbies for US Base to Close

WASHINGTON (AP) October 28, 1991 - U. S. naval authorities are seeking a former sailor, now in his 60s, in connection with the nation's worsening relations on its Pacific island territory, Guam.

A reliable Navy spokesman identified the man as Gene C. McDougall, who served on Guam during the 1950s and is believed to be living in Illinois. "It takes a long time for good relationships to deteriorate noticeably, thus we are only now able to pinpoint McDougall's ominous role in the current mess," the spokesman explained.

In this unprecedented intergenerational scenario, the authorities are apparently dismissing "statute of limitations" and "civilian status" issues. "McDougall's involvement is too obvious and heinous to be overlooked," the spokesman stressed.

"His unseemly conduct among the Guamian population precipitated a long spiral of embarrassing incidents from which our nation may never recover. We shall find this man and prosecute him to the fullest extent of military and civil law."

Gene McDougall
loner, misfit, loser

October 31, 1991

Dear Clarence,

I need your help. You have probably seen the recent press release linking my tour of duty on Guam more than 40 years ago with current worsening relations between that territory and the U. S. Government.

First of all, I want you to know that the minor incidents in which I was involved have been blown out of proportion and cannot be proved. The night I spent with the 18-year-old Guamanian waitress was merely an effort on my part to gain an insight into the local customs. It was truly an enchanted evening in a jungle cottage on stilts, her parents in the adjoining bedroom and her younger brother sharing our bedroom. It was a warm and charming experience I have always cherished, only slightly tarnished by the pistol-waving civilian construction worker who blocked my jeep as we were driving back to Agana the next morning. Since I was unarmed, I felt obliged to accept his forcefully stated position that she belonged to him.

I will not even go into the other allegations against me, since they have not been specifically spelled out. Instead, there have been innuendoes by an anonymous "spokesman."

Such leaks are reprehensible, since their very nature invites the masses to let their maginations run wild and assume I am guilty of all the legendary sexual excesses attributed to Scottish men throughout the ages. As the victim of such stereotyping, I have been harmed.

I have tried to keep a low profile these past 40-odd years, even to the extent of staying away from the net after hitting a perfectly good approach shot. I have also been careful to always take a lot of the pace off my serves. This has resulted in my having served only one ace in 1991. (The ball bounced twice before the receiver could run up to it.) What I am asking is that, if anyone inquires about me, you simply say you don't know me. I don't feel this is much to ask, since many people have done that for me without my even asking them to do so.

And you would not be doing anything unpatriotic, since the charges against me are unfounded – and besides, they happened a long time ago and I have changed.

Thank you,

Gene

Montmorency J. Tillinghast '93

November 22, 1991

Dear Uncle Randy,

Due to overzealous promotion, overzealous assistance from peers and an overzealous computer, I find I have four dates for an upcoming dance at my college. All are voluptuous girls with superior IQs.

- One is the daughter of my father's boss.

- One is a neighbor who is a close friend of the family.

- One is tutoring me so I can stay eligible for basketball.

- And one is the homecoming queen who clearly has the hots for me, a situation I do not wish to compromise.

My friends say you have all the answers, thus I turn to you in my hour of stress. Please respond soon. The dance is in just two weeks.

Desperately,

Montmorency

Uncle Randy
advisor to the wretched

December 4, 1991

Dear Montmorency,

Please excuse the delay in getting back to you but, although your plight is certainly tragic, it was not at the top of my priority list. Try to understand that this is a world full of starving children, homeless people, crime victims and politicians - all of whom represent serious problems which I must address.

But now let us press on to your specific problem - having four dates for the same dance. First of all, the two week deadline you gave me did not allow enough time for me to give you a sensitive and well-thought-out solution before the dance. And do not think me fool enough to fall into the obvious trap you were setting for me. Oh no, Montmorency, I am not so naïve that I did not immediately see through your transparent attempt to get me to take two of these girls off your hands - the obvious result being two menages a trois. You would thereby end up being in the good graces of all four women - not only the two with whom you kept your date, but also the other two who, thanks to you, were able to get to "know" Uncle Randy.

Well, I've been around the block and am not so easily taken in, my friend. I have not been on a blind date since 1956, when I was roped into a date with a "voluptuous" woman who turned out to be – well, let's just say that anything can be overdone.

Also, in all candor, I must admit that the AIDS scare has made me much more nervous about casual sex than heretofore. In fact, l am wearing a condom even as I type these words.

However, I do not want you to think I would turn my back on you in your hour of need. Even though the dance is over, I assume you still have the four women in your life. This means that you may find yourself in a similar predicament in the future. So that you will have help the next time you overbook yourself I have taken the liberty of forwarding your letter to my good friend, Rod Everhard, who is not as skittish as I am about blind dates. He will be getting in touch with you as soon as he is released from the clinic.

Best wishes,

Gene

Chapter 3
1992 & 1993

Tennis, mail fraud, high school reunions, the S&L scandal, investing, cults, Waco, Minnesota and a pitiful cry for help from Hortense Snavely.

Hortense

Montmorency J. Tillinghast '93

January 13, 1992

Dear Uncle Randy,

You may be a genius, but you have got me in all kinds of trouble with my four girlfriends.

I took your recent advice, and three of them beat me up. The fourth girl is only 4-10, weighing 91 pounds, and through guile and dirty play I was able to salvage a draw with her. Despite all this, I remain loyal to you and your dogma. Certainly your price is right. Thus I have psyched up to give you another chance.

Here goes:

Tennis Player A is primarily a baseliner, seldom electing to go to the net and eternally ruing the moment when he might be drawn there. His rhythm is best maintained when he remains at the baseline no matter how the point is developing. In addition, he has statistics showing generally negative consequences when he departs from this regimen. Now on the point at issue he slams a perfect drive to Player B's deep backhand corner, wrong-footing said opponent to the extent that he is 10 feet away from the slashing ball at impact.

Should Player A consider departing from long-established dogma and follow said perfect drive to the alien net?

I look forward to hear your expert, insider reply.

In continued confidence,

Montmorency

Uncle Randy
advisor to the wretched

January 28, 1992

Dear Monty,

Frankly, I am suspicious. Your "hypothetical" tennis question could be construed as a criticism of the style of play employed by my good friend Gene McDougall, erstwhile nationally ranked USTA player and current holder of the coveted Paddock 65-and-over singles championship.

Up to this point, his penchant for rushing the net has been tempered by his mature realization that this should only be done in conjunction with an adequate approach shot, which he has not yet incorporated into his otherwise impressive array of weapons. These include the dreaded "McDougall fronthand" as well as the widely feared "drop-serve," which has been honed to perfection by this gifted performer and is yet to be successfully emulated by players in either the amateur or professional ranks.

I am giving you the benefit of the doubt by assuming that your question was not a dig at this tennis legend since you did say that player A had slammed "a perfect drive to player B's backhand corner." As we all know, Gene McDougall does not have that particular shot in his bag of tricks. However, I did ask Gene whether he would consider coming to the net under the very hypothetical circumstances you described, and he advised me that, since you had stipulated that player B was ten feet away from the slashing ball as it impacted in B's deep backhand corner, attacking the net would have been pointless at that juncture, since the point was over as soon as the ball touched the court out of reach of player B.

Rather than wasting his time and energy approaching the net, player A would be better advised to spend that glorious moment flashing a smug grin at player B and the admiring throng.

Hoping this solves your problem so that you can now get on with your life,

Uncle Randy

FBI, Washington, D. C.

March 22, 1992

Dear Mr. McDougall,

It has come to the attention of the Bureau's Fingerprint and Cryptography Division that someone using your typewriter and the name "Rev. Elton Jones" is making unlawful solicitations through the mails.

Since this activity crosses state lines, it is in clear violation of various federal statutes, notably the Consumer Protection Act of 1959, prohibiting use of the mails to deceive, defraud, debase, debauch, defame, defile, degrade, delude, demean or deprave as well as the promotion of wild-assed schemes with clearly no promise of success.

Our records show that you have led a generally exemplary life and that you served your country well at faraway stations. Therefore please take this as a first-offense warning, as an exhortation to transgress no more and as an expression of hope that you re-examine your values and priorities.

Sincerely,

H. J. Hallstrom

cc:
Justice Department
US Postal Service
Circuit-Riding and Itinerant Preachers Society (CRIPS)

Reverend Elton Jones
God-fearing American tax-payer

March 27, 1992

To: H. J. Hallstrom, FBI

Sir:

There are two things that really burn my ass - a three-foot high fire and shoot-from-the-hip letters such as yours that have been written for no other reason than to meet your monthly quota of harassment letters to the hard-working, honest American citizens who pay your salary.

First of all, your snide remark about my using Gene McDougall's typewriter to make unlawful solicitations invalidates all of your charges because everyone knows that Mr. McDougall does not even own a typewriter. He uses a computer.

Second, you accused me of wild-assed schemes with "no promise of success." Think, man, THINK! If no promise of success was made, how can anyone receiving such a letter possibly be deceived or defrauded?

If, on the other hand, your phraseology "no promise of success" is meant to convey your own conviction that my lifelong mission to bring goodness and decency to a world rife with hate and evil is doomed to failure, then I can only conclude that you and your Godless kind are more to be pitied than scorned. To live a life devoid of hope or faith in the ultimate redemption of the human spirit is its own punishment.

On behalf of all God-fearing people everywhere, I will pray for you, low-life weasel that you are.

Respectfully,

Elton Jones

Reverend Clarence Klotz

May 14, 1992

Dear Brother Elton,

I'm in the Carolina hinterlands tonight, hard by the Old Appalachian Trail. My flocks this time are members of two venerable trade associations holding their annual conferences here - the Buggy Whip Association of North America (BWANA) and the United Producers of High Button Shoes (UPHIBS).

These industries have suffered slight downturns in recent years, but I have exhorted their people to persevere in sure and certain promise of better days ahead.

I know your work is important, but perhaps you can pry yourself loose and join me for the concluding (May 25-29) segment of this mission. The coal furnace and carbon paper manufacturers will be here that week. I can be reached at

> The Log Cabin Hostel
> Old Distillery Road
> Flat Rock, N. C.

Expectantly,

Clarence

Uncle Randy
advisor to the wretched

June 2, 1992

Dear Clarence,

The good Reverend Elton Jones has asked me to send his regrets regarding your May 14 invitation for him to join you in Flat Rock May 25-29. Unfortunately, poor Elton was injured in a freak accident. It seems he was running full tilt after a tennis ball when he attempted to make such a sharp turn that he was unable to get out of his own way, resulting in a rather spectacular collision.

Sadly, this mishap occurred shortly after his recovery from an earlier injury sustained as a result of his too literal interpretation of the "split-step".

I apologize for taking so long to contact you, but I have been very busy packing for my upcoming sojourn to the wilds of northern Minnesota. It seems that the old schoolhouse in Baudette (population 1,147) is being replaced by a new building, and all those who studied or taught there have been invited to return to celebrate the event on the 4th of July. I was a member of the class of 1947 and left town two months after graduation, never to return except for an occasional visit (the last one being 17 years ago) - so I have mixed feelings about going back.

Will the other kids beat me up again? Will any of the girls' invitations to come over and "help them baby-sit" at a neighbor's house still be open? I had always declined, being either too naive or too shy. I don't remember which.

Anyhow, it's too late now, I suppose. Still, there was that beautiful cheerleader I still think of now and then. I had such a crush on her that I hardly ever spoke to her for fear I would say something stupid. I understand she married a physician and is now a grandmother, so I have probably missed the boat there.

Another reason I did not write sooner is that I have been so busy collecting signatures to get Ross Perot on the ballot here in Illinois. I am no longer involved in that process since last week when Perot said he did not want to work with adulterers.

Again, please accept Elton's regrets. I know he would have been happy to join you if it had been possible. He holds you in high regard and always defends you whenever your name comes up.

Cordially,

Uncle Randy

Clarence Klotz
Grange Hall, Grundy Center, Iowa

September 1, 1992

Dear Brother Elton,

An upper midwesterner like you could relate to my mission tonight. I'm addressing a doughty band from the rural organization Preserve Our Family Farms (POFFS). You know the problem. Increasing bigness can mean progress, brother, that is, more good things for more people. But when you add up all the advantages and disadvantages, the small farms' demise opens the door to incalculable social and economic maladjustments.

Where does a 49-year-old fourth-generation farmer go when he has lost his land, brother? To a city slum? To a factory where they've been laying off in order of seniority? To suburbia where he doesn't speak their language and can't adjust to 75-foot lots? To an employment agency to hear a patronizing "counselor" say he's too old?

I would ask for your aid on this mission, but I know how much time your own activities take. You should get out more. Take a vacation. Enclosed is some travel information concerning Guam, a paradise island in the Pacific. It seems just your speed.

Meanwhile I ply my calling. Our country has to be in a bit of trouble when black-soil Iowa is beset with farm problems along with the related S & L thing. Persevere, I say.

Enviably,

Clarence

Reverend Elton Jones
star-crossed investor

September 21, 1992

Dear Brother Clarence,

Exciting news! It has now become clear to me that I have been given the gift of influencing not just individuals, not just organizations, not just countries - no, these are small potatoes. I have the power to affect events in entire continents and, in fact the future of the entire civilized world! Please understand that this revelation is in no way intended to demean your good work, provincial as it is. But after receiving your letter earlier this month in which you discussed Guam, Iowa farms and such, I could not help but chuckle at the contrast between the scope of your mission as compared to the awesome responsibilities I now shoulder.

I have long known that I could affect the bottom line of financial entities such as corporations and limited partnerships. The very first stock I bought more than 30 years ago, Southern Bakeries, lost 30% of its value within days after I bought it. Coincidence? Read on. Later investments in various limited partnerships often caused their complete collapse. EPS cattle, for instance, lasted only one year after my getting into it when the General Partner was revealed to have offered the IRS a $400,000 bribe - the biggest bribe ever offered to the IRS up to that time. Then there was TRP Mining, which owned a gold mine in Peru. Two years after I bought in, the mine ceased to exist – if it ever did.

These are examples of cause and effect relationships which leave no question that I have the power to make or break just about any financial organization. Yes, it works both ways - I found that I could shore up a floundering company by selling short. The latest example is a company called Videocart, whose only product is a computer screen attached to shopping carts which will advertise specials in each aisle through which the customer is pushing the cart. Not only was the concept laughable, but their losses had increased each quarter of their existence, indicating to me that the stock should be selling for less than a dollar, so I sold it short at $7.00 - and two weeks later they signed a multi-million dollar agreement of some sort with IBM which brought the stock up to $8.00 at which point I bailed out. Don't ask me any details about the IBM agreement. I am a big picture man and cannot be bothered with such details.

But all this is but a prelude to the exciting news I promised. It is now apparent that my influence is far greater than I had ever imagined. On September 3rd, I bought a large amount of the Benham European Government Bond Fund. Less than two weeks later, the greatest monetary crisis since World War II descended upon Europe. Rather than allow this situation to snowball into a worldwide calamity, I sold my shares a week ago (at the low) causing the crisis to be resolved and the fund's price to rebound.

I felt it incumbent upon me to apprise you of this power I possess so that the two of us might work together on ways to harness it for the good of mankind.

Please advise,

Elton

The Elton Jones Investment Advisory

September 22, 1992

Dear investor:

I specialize in financial market consulting, utilizing a breakthrough system perfected over a 30 year period. For just $96 per year, you will receive a complete monthly breakdown of all stock purchases and sales in my own portfolio.

By simply buying whenever and whatever I sell and selling short when I buy, you are assured of handsome profits year in and year out. My consistent losses each and every year for the past 30 years clearly show the wisdom of the "contrary to Jones" investment system. Of course, past history is no guarantee of future results - but since I obviously have not learned from my mistakes up to this point, there is no reason to believe that I will now suddenly figure out how to make money in the market. This is the closest thing to a sure thing you are likely to find!

Send your $96 to me right away. You are losing money each day you delay. I will plow your subscription fees into the market, report the results to you - and you're off to the races!

Unselfishly yours,

Elton Jones

Reverend Clarence Klotz

Oct. 7, 1992

Dear Elton,

Your poignant 550-word recital of personal rebuffs in the financial world prompts this simple, old-fashioned circuit rider to compress his philosophy into six words:

- Do good.
- Keep studying.
- Think ahead.

Meanwhile, in order that I may bet the opposite and thus make some extra spending money in the cruel, secular world, please forward your predictions on future football games, political contests and stock movements.

Finally, one of my flock offers these hot tips for your future investments: (a) high-button shoes, (b) biplanes, (c) sulfa drugs and (d) wire recorders.

Incredulously yours,

Clarence

Uncle Randy
advisor to the wretched

October 24, 1992

Dear Clarence,

It has come to my attention that the annual membership fee at your tennis club is higher for men than for women. This has so traumatized at least one of your members that he is unable to sleep at night or hold down solid food. On his behalf, I am writing to learn how you can justify such blatant discrimination.

Certainly you cannot be giving this preferential treatment to women based on their being a minority, since they outnumber men. If indeed that is your rationale, then what is your policy regarding the following groups, most of whom actually ARE minorities - at least here in Arlington Heights. Of course I am referring to Asians, Scots, Afro-Americans, homosexuals, poets, pimps, authors, pedophiles, sodomizers, adulterers and retirees.

My client, whose identity I am not at liberty to divulge, should be eligible for a discount in at least two of the categories listed above, not to mention several more, since he is also a senior citizen, a handicapped person and a military veteran who went through hell in the service of his country.

Surely he deserves some recognition for having spent 28 months as a prisoner on Guam. True, this was after the great war, but since he wanted to go home and the U. S. Navy refused to allow it, he was technically a prisoner - and he suffered greatly due to the fact that those were the years when he was at his sexual peak and men outnumbered women 100 to 1 on that godforsaken rock. If I were free to disclose his name, I'm sure you would agree that this is a man who would need much better odds than this in order to achieve any measure of success with the opposite sex.

In short, Clarence, I am asking that you send me a listing of your annual membership fees as they apply to each minority, ethnic, or special interest group. After reviewing the list, I will be happy to work with you to implement the changes needed to make the fee schedule fair and just to all concerned.

Indulgently,

Uncle Randy

Clarence Klotz

November 5, 1992

Dear Uncle Randy,

You have cited Asians, poets, Scots, Afro-Americans, homosexuals, pedophiles, authors, sodomizers, adulterers and retirees as categories of persons theoretically deserving of special consideration with respect to dues charged at the cited indoor tennis facility. Your point might seem to be well taken. However, the seemingly limitless roster of special interest groups well militates against fair, effective implementation. For example, should not transvestites, Hungarians, parolees, comedians, auto salesmen, Indonesians, riverboat gamblers, northern Minnesotans, longshoremen, ridge runners and politicians be given similar consideration under your plan? This is not an issue to be treated glibly.

As to your grievance over the 5 percent differential between men's and women's dues at the aforementioned facility, the latter's marketing, legal and public relations departments have issued a joint statement supporting the status quo. Its upshots follow:

- It's a question of supply and demand, a main plank in the tenets of you capitalists. Various court judgments have supported the right of a private club to charge what it deems proper. The club's greatest need is for daytime women, thus a mild (though fast-disappearing) discount.

- About half the club's female members are wives of male members, thus the former's dues come out of the same pocket, removing some of the sting from the "discrimination" argument.

- The women's locker room is considerably more limited than the men's, a situation not covering the owners and architects with glory. Thus an historic secondary reason for the differential.

- In keeping with published national statistics, there are more slobs among the male members, a situation resulting in greater towel usage and more difficult cleanup assignments on the men's side.

Please do not label this reply a copout or a contentious document. We always appreciate your views, however incredulous, and will fight to keep the lines of communication open. Be assured that my colleagues and I will continue to press for your election to the Lake of the Woods Hall of Fame.

A devoted reader,

Clarence

Uncle Randy
advisor to the wretched

November 26, 1992

Dear Clarence,

Thank you for your prompt and sensitive response to my October 24 letter regarding your two-tiered membership fee schedule. I accept the irrefutable logic of your marketing, legal and public relations departments. Unlike those who place hope in God or man, I am never disappointed. And I must admit that when you expressed the need for daytime women, you struck a responsive chord since I have experienced similar longings from time to time.

Moreover, as a mature individual, I rejected out of hand the first thought that came to mind - that my client might beat the system by undergoing a sex change operation. After calmly evaluating the cost of such an operation and then factoring in the annual savings as well as his life expectancy, this did not seem to be a viable option. Number-crunching really paid off that time. Just one of the rewards of a good education, and the primary reason why so many people come to me for advice and counsel.

Proud to serve,

Uncle Randy

The Venerable Reverend Elton Jones

April 3, 1993

Dear Brother Clarence,

You are cordially invited to join the cult I am putting together. I have decided to take this step because the low profile style I have employed to date has not brought about as significant a change in the world as I had hoped.

Of course I realize there are dangers in having too high a profile, as our embattled brother and his flock in Waco will attest. Yet danger is always with us no matter how meekly we go about our daily lives. We are surrounded by smokers who believe they have the right to befoul the air we must breathe, women who steal up behind us and slam their shopping carts into our Achilles tendons, teenage girls driving cars, small children all over the place - there is no escape. Or is there?

I have found some very inexpensive acreage in a remote area just outside of Baudette, Minnesota where we could build a compound for our flock (to consist of you, me and as many nubile women as can be found). That last point, finding the women, is where you come into the picture. As I am much too busy to search them out, and inasmuch as my success in converting them has not been encouraging in the past (even my newly acquired mustache does not seem to have helped), it will fall upon you to do the recruiting.

Yes, the winters will be cold and the summers full of large mosquitoes, but as stated earlier, the land is cheap. And I'm sure you are aware of the tax advantages.

Eagerly awaiting your response,

Elton

Reverend Clarence Klotz

April 8, 1993

Dear Venerable,

I feel a new lease on life. Many moons have passed since a fellow man has chosen me to recruit women, apparently in confidence that I could actually be productive in such an endeavor. It soothes the soul and puts spring in one's elderly step. However, I have reservations about your site selection. Former basketball players are well known for eternally seeking "home-floor advantage," thus we outsiders must be eternally vigilant. We are naturally leery of the mores and folkways of foreign countries, likewise the harsh demands of rustic living. Please supply further details.

Re the recruitment of women, one recalls the predicament of the infant city of Seattle in the lusty pioneer days of the Old West. The population was virtually all male, and there was no occupational balance. So they imported 400 seamstresses from the East, only three of whom owned sewing machines. While I am forever the devil's advocate, seeking only truth, justice and the betterment of humankind in the process, let us join together in protecting the good name of the good cults.

> I'd rather be a pagan tied to cult outworn
> So might I, standing on this pleasant lea,
> Have glimpses that would make me less forlorn,
> Have sight of Proteus rising from the sea
> Or hear old Triton blow his wreathed horn.

Have you been to the net lately? Life itself is a net, brother, but that's another topic for another time.

Affectionately,

Clarence

Reverend Elton Jones
the voice of reason in a world gone mad

April 23, 1993

Dear Brother Clarence,

It is my sad duty to inform you that my plans to form a cult have been canceled. Yes, I know this will come as quite a blow to you, and do not think for a moment that I do not sympathize with the disappointment you must feel. As a married man, I am certainly not unfamiliar with disappointment in my own life. Yet you can take comfort in the certain knowledge that adversity, when dealt with maturely, will inexorably enrich your life and make you a better person.

Now, let me temper your frustration with a bit of good news. I am putting out feelers to see how much interest there might be in holding the First Annual Closed Scottish Seniors Clay Court Invitational Tennis Classic Tournament this summer at the posh Hackers Haven Whirlpool Bath and Tennis Centre! By God, can you conceive of anything more eclectic?

True, I envision some problems - for instance, Irishmen might try to sneak into the tournament - but a simple IQ test could weed out such pretenders.

Let me know if I can count on your help in this grand endeavor - and please contact me if you have any questions, concerns or suggestions.

Blithely,

Elton

Clarence Klotz

May 4, 1993

Dear Brother Elton,

Your invitation to participate in a Scottish Closed Senior Clay Court Tennis Tournament is at first blush touching and profusely appreciated. However, when one factors in the number of available qualifying players for such an event, suspicion becomes rife that said event is a veiled albeit equally touching challenge to a single individual.

Might finding enough competitive Scottish senior players be the equivalent of finding a left-handed shortstop in northern Alaska? Since I am only half Scottish, do I have to give you, a higher-ranked player, a handicap such as, say, two bisque points a set? Indeed would this be comparable to the Scottish golfing experience some years ago of Barry Goldwater? When informed that the Royal and Ancient 18-hole course at hand was "restricted," Goldwater revealed that he was only half Jewish and asked if he could play nine holes. In any event, your idea has much merit. One way or another, I look forward to its application.

Affectionately,

Clarence

The Venerable Reverend Elton Jones

June 11, 1993

Dear Clarence,

After you so cruelly shot down my idea for an ethnic tennis tournament at Hackers Haven, I decided to focus on more lofty goals. As a consequence, I now find myself in Cajun country, listening to the melodic strains of "Diggy Diggy Lo" as I prepare to compete in the National Senior Olympics being held here this week.

Why should I concern myself with local tournaments when I have qualified for this national event? Would not my participation in an Arlington Heights tournament be akin to Michael Jordan's playing in a high school game? I'm sure you can see the folly in that. It is only fitting and proper that Michael and I are in Phoenix and Baton Rouge this day.

> He ne'er is crowned
> With immortality, who fears to follow
> Where airy voices lead

The fact that my chances of winning are zero does not deter me. Sure, a person could prepare for tournament competition by spending years taking lessons and developing a serve and a backhand - but where is the challenge in that?

"Far better it is to dare mighty things, to win glorious triumphs, even though checkered by failure, than to rank with those poor spirits who neither enjoy much nor suffer much, because they live in the gray twilight that knows not victory nor defeat."

Pray for me,

Elton

Female Halfway House
Backwater, Kentucky

August 19, 1993

Dear Mr. Klotz,

You don't know me but my name is Hortense Snavely and I am writing to you because in desperation I contacted Uncle Randy to see if he could find a soul-mate for me since I am a middle-aged lady and have so far not been lucky in love and according to Uncle Randy you might be just the gentleman I've been searching for since he tells me that although you are quite long in the tooth he has it on good authority that there is still spring in your elderly step which is all I ask, and in fact that would be enough to make my mother happy too because she has always hoped that one day I would marry but please don't think that's what I'm writing to you about even though, like, who knows - maybe it could develop into something and like I said before, my mother would sure like that - so now after telling you all this I might as well let you know that I am not particularly beautiful or smart but I am docile and would not be any trouble if you were to have lunch with me sometime - and I also want you to know that I chose you even though Uncle Randy gave me an extensive list of men including Montmorency J. Tillinghast whom I passed over because I understand he is a womanizer and once had a date with four different women for the same college dance while a student at a small college in rural Illinois and I also passed over H. J. Hallstrom whom I am told has a very good job with the FBI but is an asshole and then there was the good reverend Elton Jones as well as Nelson Campbell and Gene McDougall and after learning a little about those three it was obvious that for me to even contact men of such stature would be outrageously presumptuous of me so, well, I chose you and now, rather than gush on and cause you to think I am some sort of flake, I will end this and anxiously await your reply which I hope will be soon and carrying a positive message.

Warmly,

Hortense

P.S. - I want to be perfectly honest with you so I should tell you that I actually did contact Elton Jones and Gene McDougall and they both suggested that I contact you so you do come very highly recommended by a number of people.

Reverend Clarence Klotz

August 27, 1993

Dear Hortense,

We have high-minded mutual acquaintances indeed: Elton Jones and Gene McDougall for example. Inspiring leaders of thought and action, even though their positions veer from community norms at times. Friends are exultations, child. Friendship is a sheltering tree, the cement of the soul, a constant in all things, a consummation to be wished.

Mr. McDougall is a particularly outstanding character. I recently received a letter from him, the entire 34-line entity compressed into a single 412-word sentence! I am torn between attributing this to great creativity honed at the University of Minnesota School of Journalism or to negative reflections on the Baudette, Minnesota school system. In any event, I am sending a copy of that letter to the Guinness Book of World Records. The late Roundy Coughlin used to write his Wisconsin State Journal sports columns without punctuation, but Mr. McDougall has harnessed new horizons in this area.

Child, I don't mind being No. 3; "show" wins money at the racetrack, a medal at the Olympics and the mantle of contendership generally. But I am a citizen of the world, a man with limited roots, one whose missions may at a moment's notice call him to a far corner of the earth, thus militating against any mode of life that might tie him down. It is with sadness mingled with euphoria that I exhort you to look elsewhere.

As for Uncle Randy, please do not put great faith in him. For all his flowery words and seeming acumen, his success percentage at most recent survey was .087. He got lucky a few times. Meanwhile, best wishes to you from afar. Perhaps we will meet some sunny day o'er tea and crumpets. Keep the faith in the knowledge that there are many other fish in the sea, so many younger than I. O, to be 65 again...

Cordially,

Clarence

Reverend Elton Jones

November 14, 1993

Dear Clarence,

It was a pleasure to bump into you the other day, although I must confess to a certain amount of sadness as I watched you picking up refuse from the grounds at the Hackers Haven Tennis Center. I could not help but wonder how a life spent helping others could finally come down to this. And it got me to thinking. No one among us can be certain our last days will be any better. Fortunes are made and lost, health is a tenuous and capricious thing, fate is uncaring and merciless - so what can one do?

The answer, my friend, has been revealed to me, and I will share it with you right here and now. It is "look out for numero uno". Once this became known to me, my fertile mind quickly came up with a plan. You may remember my mentioning to you that I was writing a book. Well, the book will be completed by the end of this year, and it is the answer to all my hopes and dreams. You might well ask what the book is about, but that would be missing the point. Not having the writing skills of a Nelson Campbell, I will not be able to find a publisher, so I am marketing it myself. How? By mail order. Do you see the genius behind this? THE BOOK NEED NOT BE WORTH READING - THE KEY TO SUCCESS LIES IN THE ADVERTISING COPY!

By now, I know you are as excited about this as I am, but wait - I still haven't gotten to the kicker. Are you ready for this? I am offering this book for sale at one million dollars per copy. Sure, I know I am not going to sell many copies at that price, but if I sell JUST ONE, I'll be set for life.

And before you conclude that I am being unrealistic, let me put that notion to rest immediately. I fully realize that this will be a hard sell. A small ad in the Tribune classified section is not going to cut it. No, it takes big money to make big money, so I am selling my home, car and all other personal possessions in order to raise enough capital for this project. As you can see, this has been carefully thought through.

Well, Clarence, there you have it. No longer can I be dismissed as a fatuous old fart. I am sure you now realize I am more than that.

Proudly,

Elton

Reverend Clarence Klotz

December 19, 1993

Dear Elton,

I have been studying at length the plan to market your book at one million dollars per copy — in the knowledge that if only one is sold, you'll be in clover. The math works out and I'm sure P. T. Barnum would approve, but I feel there's a flaw in the scheme somewhere.

Still, remember you always have my blessing in your various undertakings, however bizarre they may be.

I was not a whit embarrassed at having you see me collecting refuse at the club gate. There is dignity in honest labor, lad. Can I not contribute to the betterment of man by doing the best possible job, whether the assignment be designing spacecraft or cleaning urinals? When do we achieve real happiness, brother, and how do we know we have it? Let the words of fellow forebear Sir Walter Scott inspire and define us:

> Sound, sound the clarion, fill the fife;
> To all the sensual world proclaim:
> One crowded hour of glorious life
> Is worth an age without a name.

Thoughts to reflect upon during the festive season! Have a joyous and safe one ...but don't sell your home and car yet!

Affectionately,

Clarence

Elton Jones' helpful tips for a better 1994

1. Never act on stock tips from hitchhikers.

2. Remove shoes before bathing, showering or going to bed.

3. Put on pants before putting on shoes. Ironically, when removing these items, the reverse is true (remove shoes, then pants).

4. Mail letters in the red, white and blue boxes - not the green boxes.

5. Do not date outside your own species.

6. Never stick beans up your nose (or anyone else's). This applies to all other orifices as well.

7. Be courteous (or at least civil) to others, especially mean-looking people who are bigger than you are.

After years of painful trial and error, I have come to believe that strict adherence to the above rules will smooth out the bumps as we tumble down the stairway of life. Good luck and best wishes for a happy holiday season and a wonderful 1994.

Chapter 4
1994 & 1995

Tennis, Santa Claus, voice mail, grammar, a satanic cult and a trip to London.

Elton senses an evil presence

Reverend Elton Jones

April 9, 1994

Dear Clarence,

Why should we be in such desperate haste to succeed, and in such desperate enterprises? If a man does not keep pace with his companions, perhaps it is because he hears a different drummer. Let him step to the music which he hears, however measured or far away.

No, those are not my words, although I could have written them. It's just that someone beat me to it. I can't quite put my finger on who that might have been, but the names Adolf Hitler and Dan Rostenkowski come to mind.

I'm writing to you because I believe you to be the most literate of all my acquaintances, and perhaps the only one gracious enough to spend his time on a problem that in the grand scheme of things would have to be considered fairly minor. There are, after all, environmental, social, political and spiritual concerns in which you are known to be deeply involved, so your time is much too precious a thing to be frittered away on meaningless minutiae. Yet, as I understand it, you do not differentiate between the big stuff and the little stuff, feeling that to do so would be judgmental and not in keeping with your philosophy of life.

It thrills and delights me to know there are men of your ilk among us, and I consider it an honor and a privilege to have had this opportunity to communicate with you.

Gratefully,

Elton

Reverend Clarence Klotz

May 4, 1994

Dear Elton,

One is never so exalted as when asked a scholarly question. My trusty library reveals that the "different drummer" quotation is from the "Conclusions" chapter of Thoreau's Walden.

Did I mention in conversation that Ken Schaller and I lost the 65 doubles final at Edens to the top seeds, 6-4, 6-7 (5-7), 7-6 (7-5)? It was the qualifier for the Western playoffs May 13-15 at Lansing, Mich., but, alas, I can't go. I'm already committed to my Navy reunion in Florida. They've found another partner for Ken - in the 70s.* Ken understood that we'd play only one match the first night, so he played that morning at Barrington. Ha! We played two, 40 minutes apart, and the second one lasted more than two hours. Ken, who plays much more than I, cramped up several times later that night, and I, though feeling great, couldn't get to sleep until 4:30 a.m. How do you counteract muscle tautness?

Humbly,

Clarence

* We were the only entry in the 70s, so they asked us to play in the 65s. Have I lived that long?

Reverend Elton Jones

May 8, 1994

Dear Clarence,

I was distressed to learn that you and Ken Schaller lost your tennis match. Who beat you? They must be famous. You asked how to counteract muscle tautness. At our age, muscle tautness should be <u>celebrated</u>, not counteracted!

While on the subject of tennis, might I modestly mention that Denny DeJesu and I won the Prince Cup 3.5 doubles tournament last night at Heritage? First prize was a new pair of Prince shoes for each of us. Now we go on to play in the regional in Libertyville on August 20 for new warm-up suits.

I should also mention that they timed our serves. Sad to say, my mighty 59 mph serves of yesteryear are no more. I was clocked at 48 mph (but I hardly ever double fault). I take comfort in the certain knowledge that my serve protects me from ever being moved up from my present 3.5 rating. Playing at that skill level, my unique overhead drop shot, widely feared fronthand volley and judicious selection of partners should provide me with a continuing bounty of shoes, warm-up suits, trophies and money in perpetuity.

Life is good,

Elton

Reverend Elton Jones

May 26, 1994

Dear Clarence,

My how-to manual, Atherosclerosis, Fighting Back, has been completed and the Daily Herald featured a story on it in this morning's paper.

Already I am reaping the benefits. This morning, as I was shopping at Jewel, a lady asked me if I was the man whose picture was in today's paper. When I told her I was, she said, "How wonderful what you're doing. God bless you." She was rather matronly, but I am already planning another trip to Jewel this afternoon in hopes of meeting a more nubile type.

Tomorrow I am wending my way to South Bend where I will watch some of the NCAA tennis championships and also play in the Pie Seifert Memorial Day Open USTA 65s tournament. I called today for my start time only to learn that there are but five entries and I am the only seed. In the few instances in where I was the top seed in a tournament, I have always reacted by becoming so enamored of myself that I was soundly thrashed in the first round. God help me!

When I return, Hackers Haven's newly refurbished clay courts will await, and I hope you will consider entering the first annual Northwest Suburban Bald Authors Over 65 Invitational Tennis Tournament, which I am currently putting together. If you do, you will be either the number one or number two seed, since there will only be the two of us. Oh, what the hell - you can be number one.

Humbly,

Elton

Reverend Elton Jones

October 7, 1994

Dear Clarence,

Sorry that it has taken me this long to get around to thanking you for all your help in plugging my book, but I am a very busy man. A large percentage of my time these days is spent right here in the house alternately misplacing and searching for my pocket secretary. I need to refer to it frequently in order find out what I am supposed to do the rest of the day. Sometimes I find it too late to accomplish that day's activities, so I must postpone some things to the following day. After a while, everything begins to pile up and it gets really hard to stay organized. And I have also spent a great deal of time the past few weeks searching for my favorite sweater. Finally, in desperation, I called the motel I last stayed in - the Manor View in Springfield. Sure enough, it was there. Once again, confirmation that a life of pure thoughts and good deeds is always rewarded.

I have gone to great lengths to explain how busy I am so you will not think I waited this long to contact you out of anger over your having once again managed to avoid playing with me on the clay this entire summer, even though this now makes 23 years in a row that this has happened. My firm belief that all is well with the world and that everything will work out in its own good time continues to sustain me.

Sanguinely,

Elton

Greetings from the North Pole

December 15, 1994

We tlingits and aluets are realy imprest by yer win over wall... word reacht us by dogsled.

best wizhes in fewcher turnments.

Nanook

Reverend Elton Jones

January 3, 1995

Dear Clarence,

If you thought you could titillate me by traveling all the way to the North Pole to mail a letter just to make me think I was getting a letter from Santa Claus, think again. I quit believing in Santa many years ago. (After joining the navy, my fellow sailors quickly set me straight on that.) In other words, I've "been around the block" as they say, and am not easily taken in. On the other hand, I am not so jaded that I have lost my faith in the benevolent, omnipotent power watching over us all. After all, was he not in my corner when I played the widely feared Roger Wall? The fact that in so doing, he had forsaken poor Roger is another matter which I do not feel qualified to address since I am, after all, only a grain of sand in this vast beach of life. Suffice to say that, while I do not have all the answers, I do have an abiding faith in all that is decent and good and - yes - I am not ashamed to admit that this also includes an unshakable belief in Peter Rabbit and the tooth fairy. I can speak with confidence because I have never seen or heard a single thing during my entire 66 years of existence that disproves the existence of either of them.

But now to the purpose of this letter. Be not disheartened that your back went out in Aurora, robbing both you and Ken Schaller of the fame and prize money which would have been yours as doubles champs. While it may seem that you have been abandoned by the Almighty, do not lose faith! The best is yet to come. All good things come to those who wait. Meanwhile, now that you are at the age where you may begin losing a few teeth, I suggest that you put the next one under your pillow and hope for the best.

Your steadfast spiritual rock,

Elton

Reverend Elton Jones

March 29, 1995

Dear Clarence,

If I occasionally seem crabby, my following recent letter to the president of my condo association will give you some idea of the challenges I must face in my everyday life:

"This afternoon at 2:45 my doorbell rang. As a retired old codger, I was using this time to enjoy my afternoon nap - so I had to (1) get out of bed, (2) go downstairs and (3) open the door - only to find that the two-page Condo Association newsletter had been left between the screen and outside doors. I appreciate the fact that some selfless volunteer went out of his or her way to deliver this newsletter to me, but there was nothing in it that required immediate action on my part.

"What I am trying to say is that it was unnecessary to get me out of bed for this. I believe that almost the only people home at 2:45 on a Wednesday afternoon would be the elderly and/or infirm (i.e. retired people, invalids or those home from work because they are sick). There is a good chance that these people would be in bed. And, yes, there are also the people who work night shifts. Certainly, they would also be in bed trying to get a good day's sleep before getting up and going to work. I cannot think of any other people who would be home in the middle of the afternoon on a weekday. Newlyweds? Doubtful, but even if they were home, would they appreciate the interruption? I don't think so.

"Anyhow, I wonder if you could mention this at the next board meeting and ask that, as an act of compassion, your volunteers refrain from ringing doorbells when they deliver newsletters? Of course, I would be the first to defend their right to make exceptions in those cases when the resident would clearly benefit from being rousted out of bed. One example might be if the house were on fire. Off hand, I cannot think of another example."

Well, Clarence, there you have it – a sobering glimpse inside the personal Hell that is my everyday existence. Not a pretty thing, but a burden I accept gladly, knowing that what seems so cruel and meaningless now is all part of a greater plan which will be revealed in all its glory one sweet day.

Glory be,

Elton

Reverend Clarence Klotz

April 1, 1995

Dear Elton,

Any compassionate American would sympathize with you. Old codgers need their sleep, for it is sleep that knits up the raveled sleeve of care.

Now for my pet peeve, Elton. It is the automatic call-routing machinery numerous companies have set up, apparently to reduce labor costs: "If you wish to place an order, Press 1. If you wish to assassinate the board chairman, Press 2, etc." Have you ever obtained full satisfaction from one of these exchanges? Don't you usually wind up talking with a real live human being anyway? And wouldn't you like to see the economics of it all? If it doesn't save much money and three times as many customers are mad, how is that getting ahead?

Thanks for sharing your eloquence.

As always,

Clarence

Reverend Elton Jones
swimming upstream

June 26, 1995

Dear Clarence,

While eating breakfast this morning, I thought of an excellent answer to an insulting remark that was made to me about twenty years ago. Yes, I realize the moment has passed and it would be inappropriate to contact this individual now with my retort. Certainly there would be no spark of spontaneity remaining at this point. Yet, the realization that I am still in possession of some of my faculties has lifted my spirits and moved me to share my unbridled joy with you. Sure, I may be a little slow, but "if a man does not keep pace with his companions, perhaps he hears a different drummer: Let him step to the music which he hears, however measured or far away."

On the other hand, perhaps it was not a good thing to have allowed this unresolved issue to dwell somewhere in the dark recesses of my mind for decades. Would it not have been better to have forgotten this incident long ago? The answer to this question may come to me after a few years of incubation - or maybe not.

In the meantime, I am turning to you for counsel because you seem to have somehow achieved a balance in your life that I still seek. Whatever your secret, I hope you will share it with one less fortunate who is still searching for he knows not what.

Confused - yet hopeful,

Elton

Reverend Clarence Klotz

July 9, 1995

Dear Elton,

What more eloquent justification for a checkered life than praise from a respected peer? How better to combat self-perceptions of misspent youth? What better soothant to the savage breast than to be asked by a noted contemporary the meaning of it all?

You are troubled, but you need not be. Remember, they are the thinkers who despair most. They set higher standards for themselves, thus have more room to fall. They worry about accomplishment while others stumble through life, looking to neither right nor left. They are the doers, those on whom our country depends to pass the torch.

As one who identifies himself with too many unfinished symphonies and too many products in search of missions, let me exhort you to forget the barbs of eld. Let your superior strength blot out the indiscretions and ill-considered mouthings of lesser men. Care not what the rabble sayeth, brother. Rise above the fray. Your country, community and tennis club need you!

Affectionately,

Clarence

Reverend Elton Jones Rescue Mission

August 6, 1995

Dear Brother,

Even though it is my mission in life to give hope and strength to those weaker than I, there are times when I am faced with a problem so overwhelming that it engulfs my very being. I am not too proud to admit that now is such a time. I feel inadequate to the task before me, and must once again seek your counsel.

The problem is, is that I cannot bear listening to any more supposedly educated people using double *is*'s while being interviewed on TV. There, I just did it myself - God help me! This must be nipped in the bud. It wasn't long ago that this same crowd began using "hopefully" and "momentarily" in ways that made my skin crawl. I have almost come to accept that when someone says he will "stop by my house momentarily" he does not intend to stay just a short while, but he intends to get here right away - and that if he says he will "hopefully arrive soon" he will not arrive full of hope but only hopes that he will get here promptly. By now, I have learned to live with all that. But two *is*'s? Must we tolerate that? I would rather hear a fingernail on a chalkboard.

I would not have bothered you with this if it weren't important. Please advise.

One other irritant you might be able to alleviate. As a benevolent man of the cloth, I want to put an end to the suffering that O. J. Simpson has been forced to endure month after month at his murder trial. I wonder if you know of some way to get in touch with Marsha Clark to advise her to publicly offer O. J. a chance to have the charges against him dropped if he will simply take the stand and answer just one question - "Did you do it?" If he answers "no," he goes free. If he answers "yes," he gets life without parole. The only proviso would be that he agree to a shot of sodium pentathol before being asked the question. As a "100% not guilty" man, one would think he would jump at the chance.

Since you are better connected than I, the ball is now in your court. Good luck - and no need to give me any credit for the idea. Just the knowledge that I have helped make the world a little better place will, as always, be reward enough for me.

Piously,

Elton Jones

Reverend Clarence Klotz
Saver of Souls, Anywhere, USA

August 9, 1995

Dear Elton,

Once again you have struck tender chords. We men of the cloth perhaps have a special knack for that. I share your abhorrence for the verbal abominations you cite. My peeves are in the following order, with yours coming next:

"Ya know?"

"Basically"

"You know what I'm saying?"

"Went" as past participle of "go"

Recently I caught a young radio interviewee cramming 18 "ya knows" into a one-minute commentary. This should be at least near the District and Western records. Do you know the national record? To a litigant who ended a statement with "ya know," TV's Judge Wapner replied, "No, I don't know. That's the reason we're having the trial." A political candidate recently said he didn't want "to cast any aspirations" against his opponent but thought he was being extremely unfair. A high-paid newscaster reported that the police were cracking down on "pickpocketers." One TV interviewee said that Americans have too many hang-ups. "They're too inhabited." Another said his ex-boss was up on "tax invasion." Another told of Latins' penchant for gala "fiascos."

Spelling is another peeve, brother. Why can't our fellow journalists look up the tricky stuff? In his current "Writer's Art" column, J. J. Kilpatrick cites one newspaper's usage of "Pontius Pilot," another's identification of a bookstore person as "a graduate student in Midevil Studies," and classifieds advertising a "soup terrain" and a "sub-merciful pump." Speaking of high-paid newsfolk, will they ever learn the difference between "lie" and "lay?"

In mutual piety,

Clarence

UNCLE RANDY
advisor to the wretched

August 25, 1995

Dear Clarence,

A source I dare not reveal (you will understand why as you read on) has informed me of a recent sighting which fills me with grave misgivings. A mutual friend of ours, Nelson Campbell, was seen at the Hackers Haven Tennis Resort playing with one Ken Schaller and both men were wearing what appeared to be sailor hats! Since such headwear has seldom been seen anywhere in the past decade or so, and since not just one, but both men were seen wearing these hats, coincidence can be ruled out. This leaves us with the obvious conclusion that both men are members of a secret society of some sort. Simple logic compels me to deduce that if the society is a secret one, there is something nefarious about it. It therefore follows that they may very well be devil worshipers. I don't want to believe this, but what other conclusion can be reached?

My informant has been so shaken by this ominous discovery that he has come to me for counsel. The implications of what he observed have chilled him to the bone, and he has been unable to hold down solid food or sleep other than in the fetal position since that time. Worse yet, he is afraid to go back to Hackers Haven. Although I have had great success in helping those who are mentally and emotionally troubled, my skills have not been equal to the task in this instance - thus, I am turning to you. As a man of the cloth, perhaps you can reach beyond where I can go to help this forlorn creature.

God help us all,

Uncle Randy

Reverend Clarence Klotz

September 4, 1995

Dear Uncle Randy,

The "sailor hats" to which you younger fry refer are, of course, "Rod Laver hats," a tribute of sorts to the most recent male Grand Slam achiever. Ken and I represent an older age group, thus our mores and folkways may be difficult to fathom.

But there are other factors favoring our headwear:

- They grip the head better than caps.

- They con a few uninitiated spectators into thinking we might have been in Laver's class long ago.

- They're still on hand and not yet threadbare, thus preclude the necessity of buying new ones.

A secret society? Thanks for the idea. We would never have been so resourceful. Please relax, get some rest, renew your spirits and

Keep the faith,

Clarence

Reverend Elton Jones

September 25, 1995

Dear Brother,

As I get older, I am becoming increasingly aware of the need to compensate for the rotation of the earth when I swing at tennis balls. As if this weren't enough, I am now finding it necessary to factor in an additional item - the alarming yet indisputable fact that while the earth is constantly orbiting the sun, <u>it is also spinning on its own axis!</u> There is more involved here than just hitting a tennis ball properly. Do you realize that if it weren't for gravity, we'd all be flung off into space? Since most people are unable to grasp this concept in the first place, they go blissfully on their way each day as if nothing untoward were taking place. But with my keen insight, staying calm is becoming a greater challenge all the time. Frankly, sixty-six years of fighting all this is starting to take its toll. By "all this" I refer not only to this spinning and rotating problem, but also to all kinds of other stuff - like why should I have to always bear in mind that "flammable" and "inflammable" do not mean the opposite of each other as it would seem, but actually mean exactly the same thing? Does that make any sense to you? Do we need both words? I consider this just another unnecessary burden to carry around. These kinds of things pile up after a while.

Sorry to lean on you like this, but sometimes I'm not sure I can continue to carry this load alone. As always, I have turned to you in my moment of weakness in the firm belief that your strength will carry me through. I know you will not fail me. Please advise ASAFP.

Anxiously,

Elton

Reginald Q. Twillingham, Manager

Nell Gwyn House Apartments, Sloane Avenue, London, England

November 3, 1995

Dear Reverend Klotz,

Today, a quite frail and confused old man wandered into our complex and managed to convey to us that he was lost. After talking with him - or attempting to - we concluded that he was indeed lost, not only geographically, but in every sense of the word. Being Englishmen, we are decent sorts, so we have cleaned him up the best we could (he was badly in need of a bath and a shave), and have spent considerable time trying to find out who he is. There is no way to know his real name, since he gives us a different one every time we question him. One time it is Uncle Randy, then it is Reverend Elton Jones, then Gene McDougall - you get the picture.

It seems this poor unfortunate was on his way to your Hackers Haven Tennis Centre and took a wrong turn. The story gets fuzzy after that, but he seems to know someone there. Your name was mentioned along with others such as H. J. Hallstrom and Montmorency J. Tillinghast.

Needless to say, this man needs help, and we desperately await any information you can give us about him. We do not want to keep him around very long, since we find his manners and habits offensive. As a matter of fact, we plan to send him back to the colonies November 10, whereupon he will become someone else's problem.

Disgustedly,

Reginald

Reverend Clarence Klotz

November 14, 1995

Dear Elton,

My mind is swirling. When I served, I was already compensating for barometric pressure and phases of the moon. Now you want me to factor in rotation of the earth! I hope my 67-mph bomb doesn't suffer in the process.

Then, as if that that burning issue weren't too much to bear, comes a letter from one Reginald Q Twillingham in far-off England regarding a person strongly fitting your description. At least he was "frail, confused and unkempt." Wily old manipulator that you are, would you have pulled this "lost on another continent" caper for publicity, perhaps to increase sales of your book? Why shouldn't men of the cloth be permitted an antic or two?

In the late 1930s one Douglas "Wrong Way" Corrigan set out to fly his private plane from New York to California but wound up in Ireland. He, too, said he was confused. Ha!

Columbus proved you could sail west to get east. Why couldn't one keep going east to get west, arriving back at headquarters via, say, Samarkand, Singapore, San Francisco and Schaumburg? Meanwhile my attorney says I have no recourse but to sue you. I laughed so hard at the Twillingham letter that I wrenched some stomach muscles and was unable to take food for hours. I'm sure you'll understand.

Impressed,

Clarence

Reverend Billy Bob (Hoss) Gonzales
Inter-Faith Refuge for the Homeless

December 19, 1995

Dear Reverend Klotz,

We have a very unhappy situation here that I pray you can help us resolve. As you may know, we are known throughout the world as the last refuge for the most wretched of all mankind. The dregs of humanity who have been cast out everywhere else very often end up here and we cheerfully take them in and give them the care and love that could possibly turn their lives around.

However, we now have a case which we consider unique. Newly arrived among us is a bedraggled transient calling himself "the venerable reverend Elton Jones" who (trust me on this) gives new meaning to the word "loser." He admits to having been shunted from one place to another to the point where he now considers himself the dry land version of the Flying Dutchman, and claims to have been unable to find happiness, peace or acceptance in such disparate places as Guam, Minnesota, England and your Hackers Haven Tennis Center. In short, he just has not been able to fit in anywhere.

Frankly, Reverend Klotz, we do not feel that he fits in here either. I will not go into the details of his appearance or behavior. If you know him (as he says you do), you are all too aware of what I am talking about.

Please do not misunderstand. We are not unsympathetic to his plight. It is just that we are simply not set up to help this type of individual. What would you do with a person who, shortly after you mercifully take him in off the street, tries to induce your flock to overthrow you and establish a cult which sacrifices virgins?

Please, in the name of God, take him back! He says that he has paid membership dues there, so we really feel that he is your responsibility, not ours. Mindful of how unseemly it would be to toss his sorry ass out during the Christmas season, we will keep him until the 30th of this month - then back he goes! Sorry, but we have our own people to consider, and he is getting under their skins. I know you will understand.

Impatiently,

Hoss

Chapter 5
1996

Grammar, the homeless, publishing, tennis, sophistry and writing.

*Wannabe author Terrance Twitherspoon
must first overcome writer's block.*

J. P. Kennedy Rockefeller
for the partnership

January 1, 1996

Dear Hoss,

These are indeed times that try men's souls. No matter how broad, how deep or how soft the safety net, there are always a few among us who can't or won't cope. These are people who, for reasons of inability, disability or general meanness, are left by the side of society's road, awaiting the Good Samaritan, the Grim Reaper or a con target.

Apparently one of these unfortunates, or untouchables, is the "Venerable" Reverend Elton Jones. What can we of civilization do for a man who has been unable to find a niche in even such woebegone hinterlands as Guam or northern Minnesota?

While I do not blame you, a professional marketer, for trying, you surely cannot expect Hackers Haven Tennis Center to take back Elton straight up. The risks under any scenario are great. However, if you will throw in additional properties, say, light bulbs, old tire chains or white tennis balls, we will consider negotiating. We look forward to hearing from you.

Navidad Felicitas,

J.P.

P.S. Sacrifice virgins?!!

Reverend Billy Bob (Hoss) Gonzales
Interfaith Refuge for the Hopeless

January 5, 1996

Dear Reverend. Klotz,

Although Reverend Elton Jones, about whom I complained to you two weeks ago, has now been cast out and therefore poses no further problems to me or my flock, I continue to be troubled. I am tormented from within because I now realize I was not totally honest with you or myself. Nothing so tortures the soul as a betrayal of one's own values. Please permit me to unburden my heavy heart by confessing to you how petty, childish and spiritually dishonest my letter to you actually was.

It was not his attempt to overthrow me and set up a religion based upon the sacrificing of virgins that prompted my letter to you, nor was it his unkempt appearance or any of the other things about which I complained. The truth is, I could not abide the holier-than-thou attitude he demonstrated when I or any member of my congregation attempted to engage him in conversation. What particularly sticks in my craw is the time I innocently observed that he "was different than the rest of us" whereupon he became very agitated and loudly, with arms flailing wildly, announced that "No, no, no - it is different FROM, different FROM, not different THAN." When I pointed out that such prominent journalists as Tim Russert used "different THAN," he said he "didn't give a rat's ass." Frankly, hearing a fellow man of the cloth express himself so crudely really pissed me off.

This was a hard letter to write, Reverend, but I feel that I am a better man for it. I feel cleansed, if you will. Should I ever again be faced with a challenge such as that presented by Reverend Elton Jones, I pray I will be better prepared. To be charitable, let me say in conclusion that I do not believe him to be an evil man. He was probably sent here for a reason - perhaps to test our reaction to someone so annoying. In that sense, his sojourn amongst us could actually be considered a positive learning experience.

Praise the Lord.

Hoss

Reverend Clarence Klotz

January 10, 1996

Dear Hoss,

You are to be commended for your selfless efforts on behalf of that hapless, hopeless, helpless wanderer, Reverend Elton Jones. Some mountains are hard to climb. But even though the world be in flames, I must take time out to agree with Elton's basic thesis. Who can discount a national irritation at grossly incorrect usages of "different than?" Will we ever find relief from this abomination? Is there any hope for those erring, high-salaried newscasters who are making more than all members of our Minnesota and Illinois journalism classes put together? Try using "differentiation" rather than "different" in this context: "differentiation than?!!!"

Also dismaying in this view is substitution by those same heavy hitters of "lay" for "lie." How many times have you heard on the tube that the victim was "laying on his back" or that the injured gridder was "laying motionless?" As for the expression "don't give a rat's ass," it must be inching its way into our lexicon. It was recently used on prime time TV by that master of tact and diplomacy, Steve McMichael.

As an original Man of the North, you may particularly appreciate a memorable sportscaster gaffe of recent vintage. Commenting on Atlanta's upcoming invasion of Green Bay, he allowed as how "the southern-based Falcons won't enjoy playing on the frozen rotunda of Lambeau Field."

Back to Elton, perhaps you're right in that he didn't just appear; he was sent. As for Sun City, forgive me for assuming even for a moment that it's a nudist colony.Count your blessings amid the strife, Hoss, remembering that you have kindred souls in faraway climes.

Keep the faith,

Clarence

Terrance (Bulldog) Twitherspoon
Public Library (temporary day residence)

January 22, 1996

Dear Reverend Klotz,

I have been told by a mutual friend, Reverend Elton Jones, that there would be no better person than you to consult on matters literary. I am a writer, and although I am going through a rather dry period right now, I have an idea that I would like to run by you.

At the outset, let me make it clear that I am not motivated by money. In spite of the fact that I am temporarily sleeping in the library, life has been good to me - and I just want to give something back. How best to do that? Give joy to children, of course.

I am therefore writing a children's book of fables. This book is the love of my life, representing more than 25 years of dedicated writing, rewriting, studying, researching and learning my craft - often skipping meals when I was too poor to afford food or too busy preparing myself for what I have now come to believe is the task I was put here on earth to accomplish.

Enclosed is a copy of the manuscript. As you can see, there is only one page so far, but I take writing very seriously and do not believe a work of art can be rushed. Each word, each phrase must be painstakingly created, with careful attention to every nuance so that all parts become wedded into one glorious experience. I hope the enclosed manuscript will give you a feel of my work so that you can recommend which marketing strategy would be best. Please advise.

Thank you,

Terrance

Clarence Klotz

January 27, 1996

Dear Bull,

I am in receipt of the literary fruits of your "glorious experience."

Though one page does not a best-seller make, you show an undeniable touch of talent, that is, in comparison with other writers living in libraries. Your speed of creativity, however, needs cranking up. If you have produced only one page in 25 years, that's only two single-spaced lines a year or only one word every two weeks.

Before trying the book publishing houses, I suggest you first become published in a magazine, thus to bolster your credentials when you do hit the big boys.

I hope this letter reaches you. A colleague of mine lived at a library unnoticed for two months. He bunked behind the "Pre-Historic Life Insurance" stacks. Until the day he was discovered, even the janitor never passed by.

Inspirationally,

Clarence

RÉSUMÉ of Gene C. McDougall
March 19, 1996

JOB OBJECTIVE: Tennis Teaching Pro

EXPERIENCE: Defeated many noted tennis players, some of whom are:

- Beeson, Joe (doubles - we hit only to his partner, even when he was alone at the net)
- Blose, Bob
- Blose, Simone
- Conrad, Fred (Circa 1975)
- Converse, Irv
- French, Paul
- Schaller, Ken
- Zumph, Rob (okay, so he was a child at the time)

Almost none of the above wins was particularly recent, but to get hung up on the time element would be missing the point. Does the fact that Joe Louis' whipping of Max Schmelling occurred more than 50 years ago detract from the magnificence of the accomplishment? Of course not! Enough said.

SPECIAL TALENTS:

Your members will have the benefit of learning shots they will never see on TV no matter how many grand slam tournaments they watch. Only I can show and teach the dreaded McDougall drop-serve or overhead drop shot. There is also the patented McDougall fronthand, which has been a feature of my game throughout the years. Does your Mike Haber possess this shot? I think not.

EDUCATION:

1947 - Was graduated 17th in a class of 23 from Baudette High School, Baudette, MN (Expelled during senior year for taking unauthorized senior skip day with four other students and then refusing to make up the time, but allowed back into school after two weeks when the entire junior class, half the sophomore class and a number of freshmen and eighth-graders staged a sympathy skip day.)

1955 - Received BA from the University of Minnesota without incident except for the one night spent in jail because of an altercation with the local police. This should not impact my suitability for the position, since it was no more serious than the incident involving Pat Buchanan who has since been rehabilitated to the point where he was briefly considered for the Presidency of the United States, mostly by those who favored his stand against the teaching of evolution in our public schools. But there just weren't enough book-burners among the electorate to make his candidacy viable.

OTHER:

To be discussed at the interview

Nelson Campbell

March 23, 1996

Dear Gene,

As spring unlocks the flowers, the hillsides start to green again and the voice of the turtle is heard in our land, this old war-horse is preparing his annual spring revival circuit. Officially it's the Spring Circuit Revival Across the Midwest (SCRAM).

I implore you to consider being co-director. The pay is minimal, but the rewards are great. I'll need to know by April 15.

Meanwhile, brother, do you not see a dramatic parallel between my movement and your tennis game? Do you not equate the bloom of the crocus, and the general renewal it portends, to the potential for a faster serve or the eternal, burning challenge to go to the net once or twice a week?

Forgive the brevity here. I am off to tend to one of my flocks. O, how this spring of love resembles the uncertain glory of an April day! Do let me hear from you.

Collegially,

Nelson

P.S. – Your gripping, provocative résumé was received after this letter was written. Let us say it will receive all the attention it deserves. Be secure in the knowledge that the recipient, who boasts an indirect win over Bobby Riggs, empathizes with you. At the height of his career, Riggs lost to Charley Shostrom of the University of Chicago, and I defeated Shostrom.

If you quiz me closely, and I hope you don't, you will learn the whole truth. The matches were 29 years apart, 1939 and 1968, and Riggs' loss was a semi-fluke. He was known for brinkmanship - letting his opponent get off to a lead, then nipping him at the end. Against Shostrom, his ploy just got out of hand.

You say you have a "patented fronthand?!!"

Have you heard that the anti-evolution candidate is a loose Buchanan the deck?

THE REGENTS OF
THE MCDOUGALL INSTITUTE

ON RECOMMENDATION
OF THE FACULTY

HAVE CONFERRED UPON

NELSON CAMPBELL

THE DEGREE OF

MASTER OF SOPHISTRY

For his masterful twisting of his 1968 win over the University of Chicago's Charley Shostrom and Shostrom's earlier 1939 fluke win over Bobby Riggs into a personal indirect victory of his own over Bobby Riggs. This is a tribute, not only to his tennis artistry, but also to his indomitable spirit and determination in refusing to deal with reality on anything but his own terms, and is in keeping with the finest traditions of the McDougall Institute.

Gene McDougall
magnificently marginal

March 26, 1996

Dear Nelson,

Your flowery prose almost seduced me into accepting the co-directorship of your upcoming spring revival circuit (SCRAM). Only upon sober reflection did it become painfully obvious that, beyond stating that the "pay is minimal" and the "rewards are great" you told me not a whit about your tour or my function as co-director. For all I know, I would be expected to do manual labor such as putting up the tents at each new location - or, worse yet, serve as a geek (one who bites the heads off live chickens). Please understand that I am not accusing you of anything. I am simply saying that I cannot possibly make an informed decision with so little information.

Skepticism is a healthy thing, and I am sure you will not be offended by it any more than I was offended by the note you forwarded regarding my March 19 job application for the position of tennis teaching pro at Hackers Haven. In it, your reference to my "patented fronthand" seemed to suggest that this shot was a figment of my imagination. As a non-confrontational person, I have chosen to ignore that unfair and unfounded innuendo.

I did find one phrase in your note quite troubling, and that was the promise that my application would "receive all the attention it deserves." At the risk of seeming paranoid, this did not give me good vibes.

Nervously,

Gene

Nelson Campbell

April 1, 1996

Dear Gene,

O, how I hate to admit it, but your description of "the fronthand" has convinced me.

Thousands of hard-working Americans will recognize it, including Don Bradley, who serves with a Western grip, and the undersigned, whose groundstrokes have been described as "Southwestern."

If the word "fronthand" isn't in our lexicon, perhaps it ought to be. Indeed, what is the natural and logical opposite of "backhand?" Certainly not "forehand." How about a national campaign? Billboards, magazines, TV?

There are times, brother, when new thinking transcends conventional wisdom. This is one of those times. Hang in there!

Tenderly,

Nelson

Terrance (Bulldog) Twitherspoon
Boxtown, IL

April 7, 1996

Dear Reverend Klotz,

Forgive me for not answering your January 27 letter sooner, but I have been busy not only working on my book, but also moving out of the library to my new quarters - a large cardboard box in an industrial area not far from your tennis club.

I realize your book marketing advice was well-meaning and offered free of charge, but frankly, I was disappointed. Although I sought your council as a wordsmith rather than a mathematician, surely you must realize that since I am not a prolific writer, I would be pushing the envelope life-expectancy-wise if I tried to get published in six different magazines one at a time before even approaching the book publishing houses. At the rate of one page every 25 years, I don't feel that I have a lot of time to waste trying to get published in magazines. Certainly you are not suggesting that I embark on a reckless race against time, sacrificing not only the quality of my work but also my very soul in the process.

Please do not think me ungrateful - it's just that I have become rather churlish of late. My cardboard box, even though it is the nicest one in the neighborhood, has not been holding up well in the rain and I am afraid I may have to move again. I had hoped that my current location would afford me the opportunity to put down some roots, raise some corn, keep a few chickens, take a wife, sire some children and leave more to the world than just my writings.

The sad fact is that without progeny, I will be the last Twitherspoon. A sobering thought, I'm sure you will agree.

Perhaps my dreams are so illusive because I set my goals too high, yet I will not knuckle under. As H. L. Mencken said, "It takes a long while for a naturally trusting person to reconcile himself to the idea that after all God will not help him."

Bloodied but unbowed,

Terrance

Terrance (Bulldog) Twitherspoon
Transient Arms Hotel, Minneapolis, Minnesota

June 4, 1996

To: Clarence Klotz

Dear Mr. Klotz,

Since I have not heard from you since I wrote to you on April 7, I can only assume that you were offended when I rejected your advice that I put my book publishing dreams on hold in favor of the lesser goal of being published in magazines.

Well, this is to inform you that your advice was not completely ignored after all. I have decided on a new career path. No longer will I chase the impossible dream. Instead, I have decided to funnel my energy and skills into a more commercially viable enterprise - sports writing. From here on out, I'm going after the big bucks. Sure, it's a sellout, but I make no apologies. Survival is the most basic instinct of every living thing.

I am now aggressively pursuing the biggest story around - Gene McDougall's bid for the tennis triple gold medal (doubles, mixed doubles and singles) in the Minnesota Senior Olympic Games currently underway right here in Minneapolis. Why do I consider this story so big? Glad you asked.

First, let me point out that McDougall arrived here to do battle completely unarmed (no serve whatsoever and a practically non-existent backhand),

and as if this weren't sportsmanlike enough, he intends to play with a torn Achilles tendon that has kept him off the courts for weeks. Truth be known, he is in no condition to even leave the house without a walker. It should also be noted that the tendon would never have been torn if he had simply laid off tennis for a while after he originally strained the tendon. Not very bright, you might say. True - but oh, so magnificently macho!

Contrast that, if you will, with another sports figure, O. J. Simpson. Here is a man who decided to murder a woman he outweighed by a hundred pounds. Yet even though he was athletic and strong enough to have won the Heisman trophy, he could not summon the courage to engage in this encounter without first arming himself with a knife and waiting for the cover of night to insure the element of surprise.

Comparing these two individuals should make it clear why I chose to be in Minneapolis this week covering McDougall rather than going to a golf club somewhere to cover Simpson's latest athletic endeavor.

Thirty,

Terrance

CLARENCE KLOTZ

June 23, 1996

Dear Bull,

I am puzzled by the classic oxymoron in your June 4 letter. You are going after the big bucks via sports writing?!! As one who pursued that calling briefly, I can assure you they were not big. Times change, of course, but consider that when I got out of your navy and mine in 1946, I started work on a downstate daily for $42.50 a week. "It should be $40," the managing editor revealed as he put his arm around me, "but you had such a good war record."

Incidentally, the salary was for a six-day week. It worked out to 85 cents an hour. If you think I was overpaid even at that rate, please keep the sentiment to yourself.

Inexplicably, my thoughts stray back to our hero, Gene McDougall. Those of us who belong to his legion of admirers are prayerfully hoping he does no more damage to his Achilles. He should not overdo a good thing, and should be mindful of the marvelous technological age in which we live. Just a few generations ago tendon surgery meant the end of an athletic career. Not so today. And he should work on that serve! Think of the additional points he could win if he raised his speed from 59 mph to 61!

Goodnight and 73,

Clarence

GENE MCDOUGALL ELDERLY MEN'S OPEN

LOCATION	Hackers Haven Tennis Center
DATES	August 20, 21, 22, 23, 24, 25, 26, 27, 28, 29, 30, 1996
	All participants must be over 67 and have had at least four major surgeries, including at least one of the following: 1) laminectomy, 2) open-heart surgery (any type) or 3) sex change. Entry fees must be paid in cash to the tournament director. No credit cards, checks, chickens, pigs, vegetables or other types of payment will be accepted.
SCORING	Two out of three sets, one serve only, overhead smashes permitted but frowned upon - and encroachment (entering the area between the service line and the net for any reason other than to return a drop shot) will result in forfeiture of the point by the offender. No spitting allowed (drooling ok).
ENTRY FEE	$100
DEADLINE	August 15, 1996
AWARDS	Cash - $10 to winner, $5 to runner-up
DIRECTOR	Gene McDougall
REFEREE	The venerable reverend Elton Jones
NAME	_____
ADDRESS	_____

WAIVER MUST BE SIGNED BY CONTESTANT

I agree that if I have an accident of any kind, including those involving bladder or bowel malfunction, it will be my mess and I will clean it up.

SIGNATURE_____DATE_____

Nelson Campbell

August 16, 1996

Dear Gene,

The "Tournament for the Elderly" is a bit of fresh air in an aimless world, a tonic to the soul. Please send 75 entry blanks to me at once. I plan to distribute them at street corners, in nursing homes and on West Madison. I hope I'm eligible. I had a tonsillectomy at 7, hernia surgery at 57 and a doctor's office excision of a keratosis at 72. Is that enough?

I note the rather lengthy nature of your tournament. I can play only from 5 p.m. to 7:30 p.m. on Tuesdays, but I'm sure you'll find a way to accommodate me. I wish you had limited players to Kramer Autograph or similar-size old-fashioned racquets, but you can't think of everything.

This is a mild protest against the selection of the Reverend Elton Jones as referee. I feel he is too ecclesiastical, thus likely to be overwhelmed by the hurly-burly naturally attendant upon tennis tourneys, particularly those attracting old farts.

Certainly I am not seeking special treatment, but you can understand why I hope for a seed somewhere in the first 16. You know about my indirect win over Riggs. My entry data will also cite indirects over Gonzales, Trabert and Seixas. I beat Don Bradley, who beat Ziggy Mednieks, who beat Steve Morgan, who beat Bob Stuckert, who beat Gardnar Mulloy, who beat Gonzales, Trabert and Seixas. Despite this, I retain my natural humility.

Please consider not entering the tournament bearing your name. It might be embarrassing to risk a headline as follows:

McDOUGALL WINS McDOUGALL'S TOURNEY AT McDOUGALL'S CLUB

Best wishes and keep me informed,

Nelson

Reverend Elton Jones

September 12, 1996

To whom it may concern:

Those of you who submitted your entry blanks for the GENE MCDOUGALL ELDERLY MEN'S OPEN scheduled for August 20 through 30 are probably aware by now that the tournament never took place. It has fallen upon me to apprise you of the reasons:

Frankly, much of the blame can be placed squarely at the doorstep of Nelson Campbell, a good and decent man, but not without flaws. First of all, he admonished Gene McDougall, the beloved organizer of the tournament, to stay out of the competition. This cut the sensitive Mr. McDougall to the quick, causing him to remove his name from the draw. When the other players learned that their chance to play him no longer existed, many of them also withdrew. This left so few entrants that the tournament had to be canceled.

Oh sure, Nelson had requested 75 entry blanks, but he did not even try to hide the fact that he was going to distribute them only to people he was sure of beating (i.e.; nursing home residents and the like). As if that weren't enough, he also protested against my selection as referee, openly stating that he objected to me because I am a man of the cloth. Reasonable men must wonder what dark forces were at work there.

But let us not be in haste to condemn any of our brothers. I prefer to think that Nelson is basically clean and pure, but that in his zeal to win such a prestigious tournament, he temporarily lost his way. Who among us has not occasionally slipped on a cow pie in his journey across the pasture of life? Let us all open our hearts and let our wretched fallen brother know that we are prepared to welcome him back with open arms.

Forgivingly,

Elton

Applications now being accepted for a limited number of lifetime memberships in

The Elton Jones Society for the Coping Impaired

For a coveted lifetime membership, simply complete this questionnaire and, if you qualify, mail it with your check for $100 to the good Reverend Elton Jones, the Society's founder, president and beloved role model.

1. When drinking a glass of water, do you routinely splash yourself by tipping your head all the way back until the ice suddenly crashes down pushing water and ice all over your face and body? If so, give yourself one point. If you have done this at least a dozen times, add another point. More than one hundred times, no need to continue. You qualify (congratulations).

2. When urinating (this question is for men only), do you flush the toilet before you are through, but misjudge how soon you will finish - necessitating an additional flush when you actually do finish? If you have ever done this, give yourself one point. If you do it almost every time, you are accepted for membership forthwith.

3. When introduced to someone new, do you forget his/her name even before the introduction has been completed? If this occasionally happens, give yourself one point. If it happens all the time, you can quit now - you are in.

4. When introducing other people to each other, do you forget one or both names? One point if you do, two points if you always do. And if one of the people is your spouse, parent or sibling, you are granted automatic membership.

5. When you go to a different room in your house, do you stand there wondering why you went there? One point if you have occasionally done so, two points if it happens almost every day - and automatic, immediate lifetime membership if this happens when that room is the bathroom.

6. If you have a pocket secretary or wear glasses or have a favorite pencil you have to search for at least once a week, give yourself a point. Once a day - two points. Several times a day - welcome to the Society. We are proud to have you.

7. While mixing with groups of people, do you find that if you speak for more than one minute, the other people begin to talk among themselves and/or wander off before you can make your point? If so, subtract ten points - we really don't want anything to do with you either (nothing personal).

If you did not qualify for membership by scoring a home run on any of the individual questions, a total of five points on the entire questionnaire (plus your $100 check) will do the trick. If you did not make the cut, try again in a few years - your chances of success increase with age.

Elton Jones

Clarence Klotz

October 20, 1996

Dear Elton,

I have applied to my own situation the membership criteria of the Jones Society for the Coping Impaired, and I could be in luck.

My point total despite Criterion #7 is a conservative 137, which, at best, should qualify me for complimentary lifetime membership or, at worst, an adjusted dues fee of no more than $1.16.

Said point total is such that I am anxious to know how it stacks up against neighborhood, city, township, county, district, state, sectional, regional, national and international records. Please let me know.

Re Criterion #6, are there special prizes for those who have misplaced reading glasses 100 times or more?

If you're entertaining promotional suggestions for the new venture, how about a coping saw as a giveaway to each unfortunate on acceptance of his (or her) membership?

Your devoted fellow traveler,

Clarence

Reverend Elton Jones

October 29, 1996

Dear Clarence,

Congratulations! We are pleased to welcome you as an honored member of the Elton Jones Society for the Coping Impaired.

We were so impressed by the application you submitted that we have waived the entry fee and hereby grant you a lifetime membership. Especially noteworthy was the score you reported. Since we were using the honor system, and the highest possible score was 10, your claim that you scored 137 distinguishes you as either the most mathematically inept or the most morally bankrupt applicant we have thus far encountered - thereby assuring you a special place in our hearts. In short, you exemplify all we at the Society hold dear.

Please let us know if we have permission to use your name in our promotional literature. We are also considering a promotional tour in the spring and would like to know if you would be available. No gratuitous nudity is planned, although we are sure you can recognize the need for occasional brief nudity which will, of course, always be done in good taste and within the context of membership drive goals. We assume you have no anal-retentive hang-ups which will cause us problems. We want a smooth running, effective team, and we expect you to fit in and not make waves.

Do you like farm animals?

Respectfully,

Elton

Clarence Klotz

November 6, 1996

Dear Elton,

To be mathematically inept or morally bankrupt, that is the question. This is to opt for the latter. I'd like to think that my 17 years of formal education were worth something.

Thanks for the waiver. It's good to be among friends.

You may use my name in promotional literature provided you clear a few perfunctory hurdles. Simply obtain written permission from my doctor, attorney, accountant, broker, analyst, clergyman, coach, banker, dietitian, haberdasher and mechanic.

You didn't like the coping saw idea, eh?

Reverently,

Clarence

Gene McDougall
loner, misfit, loser

December 3, 1996

To: Mount Prospect Police Department

When I saw that open parking space yesterday, I thought my luck was changing - but then when I returned from seeing my cardiologist downtown, my bubble was burst. No question about it - I had screwed up. The sign was plain to see, "no parking before 10 AM". And as if that weren't bad enough, it turns out that the lot was for Mt. Prospect residents only. Not one, but two $20 tickets.

I realize that none of us can expect to journey through the pasture of life without stepping in a few cow pies along the way, but this has truly been a week from hell. It started with my unwelcome 68th birthday last weekend, then my first-round tennis tournament loss in Aurora Saturday, followed by the unspeakable horror of sitting through the Bears-Packers tragedy on TV Sunday. And then yesterday's two-ticket debacle, probably a direct result of (1) my reduced capacity now that I have become a doddering old fool of 68 and (2) my lack of familiarity with train parking lots and such, since I go downtown only once or twice a year.

It would sure ease my pain as I slide down the razor blade of life if you could let me off the hook on that second ticket. (I really had no idea that we Arlington Heights folk were not allowed there.)

In any event, you have my assurance that I will update my "how to go downtown" file to include specific instructions that future trips should be made from the Arlington Heights station.

Thanks for considering my request,

Gene McDougall

Pathetic, inexperienced, bungling, star-crossed, amateur would-be commuter.

CLARENCE:

Our friend Gene McDougall finally found a way to make his journalism degree pay off. Both tickets were changed to warnings and accompanied by the officer's best wishes for a merry Christmas. Praise the Lord.

ELTON

SHADY NOOK REST HOME FOR THE WEARY

December 7 (!), 1996

TO: Gene McDougall

FROM: Just a well-wisher

Your experience with Mt. Prospect officialdom has in one swoop renewed our faith in society, the American system, Santa Claus and schools of journalism. It's hard to be more inclusive.

Grandma Moses started painting at 78, Konrad Adenauer was first elected chancellor at 73, Churchill remained in Parliament till 90, and that great statesman, Strom Thurmond (who has been in Washington since the late Stone Age but says he's for term limits), is at least 93.

So why couldn't a sprout of 68 embark on a journalistic career? (O, to be 68 again!).

Signed:

Just

Chapter 6
1997

Moldova, grammar, sex, and some get-rich-quick schemes.

Clarence tells Elton why his door-to-door breast exam service will not fly.

Clarence Klotz

March 19, 1997

Dear Brother Elton,

With crocuses again afoot in our land, you are undoubtedly preparing for your spring circuit. I hope this catches you beforehand.

O to be in Moldova now that spring is here! O to sing again those haunting melodies; "Moon over Moldova," "The Bells of Moldova" and "Don't Cry for Me, Dear Moldova." Word has reached me that your evangelistic travels will soon take you to that Shangri-La.

Moving to our mutual avocation, do you feel that Tennis Magazine's annual "record book" issue is remiss in failing to include several important statistics? For example, the following are not included:

- Fewest times at net, season
- Fewest times at net, career
- Most moonballs, match
- Most moonballs, season
- Most moonballs, career
- Slowest average serve speed in winning match
- Longest point (time)
- Longest point (number of hits)

Please do not conclude that I'm referring to your game in any way. I am but a humble seeker of truth and joy who goes from door to door, trying to leave happiness behind him. While you prepare for the road, let me retreat into the ethereal mists of spring, there to await your response in good time.

Bountifully yours,

Clarence

Reverend Elton Jones
On tour somewhere in Moldova

April 1, 1997

Dear Brother Clarence,

Greetings from Shangri-La. Yes, my spring tour has begun. As I enjoy the spectacular beauty of the narrow tributary valleys of the Prut and Dnestr, I constantly keep an eye peeled, that I might spot a glimpse of you coming over one of the undulating verdant foothills which dot the landscape here on the western edge of the Eurasian steppe.

One reason I chose Moldova as the first stop on this year's tour is because of the widely circulated rumor that you may have been planning a trip here yourself. Yes, I have received reports that earlier this year, at Hackers Haven, you were overheard discussing Moldova with a mysterious man who spoke with a foreign accent. Some swore it was Romanian (the language spoken by ethnic Moldovans) while others felt that it sounded as though he may have emigrated from one of our own southern states. In any case, he was unquestionably not from these parts, which certainly was cause for suspicion.

Happily, your March 19 letter did reach me just before I embarked on this year's tour, and I will attempt to address each of the issues contained therein, since I am aware of how deeply hurt you were when I ignored your earlier well-meaning but impractical suggestion that coping saws be distributed to all members of the Elton Jones Society for the Coping Impaired.*

1. The songs you mentioned so fondly are favorites of mine as well, but how could we overlook the lovely "Killing Me Softly With Her Moldova?"

2. Regarding your list of Tennis records overlooked in Tennis magazine, my recent loss in the mixed doubles tournament against Jim Julian and Janet Happ brings to mind a category that might also have been considered, to wit: "six–love sets where the play was not as competitive as the score would indicate."

Your fellow seeker of truth,

Elton

---

*   Benevolent man of the cloth that I am, I felt it was kinder to ignore your suggestion than to explain that if it were implemented, it would have drained the resources of the Society to the point where the entire operation would have gone belly up. Not a happy thought.

Elton Jones lost in the big city

May 1, 1997

Dear Clarence,

Sorry to bother you with this, but I need someone to translate the enclosed letter from the First National Bank of Never. You are the only one that I feel is qualified to help me with this problem.

In a nutshell, I need to know if it would be best to leave my money in this institution, or take it out and use it to finally fulfill my lifelong dream of owning my own fire station. I realize that to have a successful fire station would be a struggle until I get established. In the beginning, before I can hire help, I will have to work irregular hours - and until I can buy a fire truck, it will not be easy to deal with some of the larger fires with nothing but my car and a fire extinguisher. Still, once I get some good press, I expect the business to grow to the point where I could consider selling franchises. Then, Nelly bar the door! My fire station empire should grow like - well, wildfire.

I am no neophyte, having been in businesses for myself several times in the past. At one time, I was a one-man band, specializing in playing at pick-up basketball games, billiard tournaments, funerals and weddings, but it never really caught on. It wasn't me - it was a timing thing. Nobody was ready for this. As proof, may I point out that, even today, no matter how many weddings, funerals, pick-up basketball games and billiard tournaments you go to, I'm willing to bet that you will never see a one-man band. I was just ahead of my time (a common problem for visionaries who are so severely gifted that they see way too far into the future).

For a while, I also ran a door-to-door breast exam service. At $10 per visit, things seemed to be going well - but, at an average of three visits per day, my startup capital of $900 ran out after just one month.

Admittedly, starting my own fire station will be risky, but I can't help but wonder how safe my money is at Never. This is tearing me apart. I need the counsel of a simple man who will not be burdened, as I am, with the ability to recognize the myriad ramifications, both good and bad, inherent in each of the options available to me.

Please advise,

Elton

Transfer of funds.

First National Bank of Never

May 1, 1997

Dear Customer:

Please find enclosed a new Certificate of Deposit. As per your maturity notice and prior letter, your Certificate of Deposit reflects that no deposits during the term will be no longer allowed any longer. Please return your old Certificate of Deposit in the enclosed postage paid envelope that is enclosed. If you have any questions, please call your nearest branch office. Thank you in advance.

Sincerely,

Milly Thilley

Milly Thilley
New accounts

Clarence Klotz

May 22, 1997

Dear Elton,

If there is any correlation between the ability of bank officials to express themselves intelligently and their ability to safeguard funds, you should drive to your bank immediately and withdraw all. Be there by the time the doors open, camping out all night nearby if necessary.

As to the rest of your May 1 letter, I am many ways torn. Certainly you are a fiery personality, which may or may not qualify you to own a fire station. And certainly you are a one-man gang, which may or not reflect your infamous experiences at pick-up basketball games and funerals. You are indeed a talent in search of a practical mission, and I fervently hope there is time enough on the clock for you to find it.

I have a possible solution: put all your current and past outrageous work ideas together into a book. If Dennis Rodman and the Mayflower Madam can produce best sellers, why can't a more versatile University of Minnesota journalism graduate, armed with oodles of creativity, produce a near-best seller? Rodman may crudely compare sex in the back seat of a car to the act on a neighbor's lawn, but only you could wax compelling on your days in a door-to-door breast exam service!

This old hand will help you as much as he can. Meanwhile consider that ancient philosophy...

> Fire from the mind as vigor from the limb;
> And life's enchanted cup but sparkles near the brim.

Think on these things, brother.

Dutifully,

Clarence

Reverend Elton Jones

June 17, 1997

Dear Clarence,

Thank you for your advice re my CD at the First Savings Bank of Never. As always, I am impressed by the poetry that accompanies your thoughts on the issues in question. Your most recent one, "Fire from the mind as vigor from the limb; And life's enchanted cup but sparkles near the brim." has caused me a great deal of pain in that I find it a tad beyond my ken. I have read it over and over again, then slept on it and read it some more - but then, just as I think I have grasped the meaning, it tragically slips from my grasp. Perhaps I could comprehend it if I were able to read the entire work in context. Or not.

I know I am here on earth to help others, but who is helping me? Obviously, God has other work which is higher on his list of priorities. I'm sure that, during the basketball season, just answering the prayers of free-throw shooters is enough to keep him so busy that my petty concerns would get lost in the shuffle. I don't mean to sound as though my faith is beginning to waver, but I have even considered changing careers. In the end, though, I always get back to the basic reason I became a man of the cloth in the first place. It is hard to beat a job where there is no work involved, the only requirement being the ability and willingness to mouth a few platitudes at the appropriate times. And there is always the possibility of big money if I were to set up a television ministry. Friends have told me that my television appearances could give new hope to those who, perhaps for the first time in their wretched lives, could enjoy a feeling of superiority.

You may find this line from a famous poem to be food for thought:

"There was a young man from Nantucket"

Warmly,

Elton

Clarence Klotz

July 7, 1997

Dear Brother Elton,

Fret not. Those who know you best know that you have redeeming features. Indeed you are frequently bracketed with those fellow storied sons of the woods, Garrison Keillor, E.G. Marshall and Paul Bunyan.

I am trying to picture you as a televangelist, but it's not working. Eltonics? Aimee Semple Jones? Just plain Elton Jones, "your friendly rock of salvation?" It doesn't sound right. No offense.

Shifting to the secular, I watched one game of your recent match with Tom Fredrickson. It consumed 8 minutes, 15 seconds. At that rate a 6-4, 6-4 match would, with just a 5-minute warmup, take 2 hours, 50 minutes. A 6-3, 4-6, 6-3 match, typical of your operations, would take just under 4 hours. Perhaps it is tiring for you just to read this.

You raised a point of context. Following is the entire stanza from which the couplet in my recent letter was taken. Not too many people in my neighborhood are concerned with Childe Harold these days. The full text helps each of us a little but perhaps not enough.

Hoping the "Nightmare of Never" is over, one way or another, I remain

Your devoted confidant,

Clarence

from
Childe Harold's Pilgrimage
by Byron, Canto iii, St.8

Something too much of htis: - but now 'tis past,
And the spell closes with its silent seal,
Long-absent Harold reappears at last;
He of the breast which fain no more would feel,
Wrung with the wounds which kill not, but ne'er heal,
Yet time, who changes all, had altered him
In soul and aspect as in age: years steal
Fire from the mind as vigor from the limb;
And life's enchanted cup but sparkles near the brim.

Reverend Elton Jones

July 23, 1997

Dear Clarence,

I am embarrassed and cannot get on with my life until I confess (although you probably are aware of my error anyhow). I'll get straight to the point. The remorse I have felt these many weeks was caused by my use of the expression "Nelly bar the door" in my May 1 letter to you. God knows (and I'm sure you know, too) that the correct expression is "KATIE bar the door". As I sink deeper and deeper into the ranks of the elderly, more of these calamities seem to befall me.

I don't know what possessed me to use the word "Nelly", unless it was an old song running through my hoary, weather-beaten bald head - "Nelly" being the only word of the lyrics that I knew.

Da da deedada, NELLY,
Da deeda, deedadada

Or from another song or poem, "Run for the roundhouse, Nelly. He can't corner you there."

But I digress. As everyone knows, "Katie bar the door" is most generally believed to have come from an old English folk song, described in the following excerpt from "The Word Detective."

"In the song, Katie and her husband are arguing, and somehow agree that the next one to speak will lose the argument. Since neither will speak to suggest barring the door at bedtime, robbers break in during the night and commit various outrages against the pair. The end of the song apparently involves the husband crying out at last and repelling the miscreants, thereby losing the argument with his wife. "

The phrase I underlined in the preceding paragraph is one that I found to be strangely compelling. I will close now so I can be alone with my thoughts.

Vicariously,

Elton

CLARENCE KLOTZ
Friend of the Friendless, Neighbor to All

July 29, 1997

Dear Brother Elton,

You needn't have been embarrassed. Having long recognized your considerable creative/literary talents, I thought "Nelly, bar the door" was simply a slick example of transference, freely understood.

Methinks thou protesteth too much.

I revel in those "roundhouse" lines; I have apparently led a sheltered life. By setting forth the stirring "Katie, bar the door" origins, you have performed a humanitarian service deserving of universal thanks.

Beyond Nelly Bly, Nellie Melba and Nellie Fox - and "Wait Till the Sun Shines, Nellie" (Number one on the Williamson County Hit Parade for 23 weeks) - this old war-horse recalls the marquee on a theater specializing in stage plays:

> NELLIE WAS A LADY
> FOR 8 DAYS
> BEGINNING SUNDAY

Keep the faith and your head high (but not when you're hitting the ball),

Clarence

Home for the nervous and perplexed

August 1, 1997

To: Clarence Klotz

Dear Clarence,

Reverend Elton Jones, whom I understand you know, suggested that I get in touch with you regarding the following problem:

I have two brothers. One works for Hackers Haven Tennis Center and the other one was electrocuted for murder. My mother died in an institution for the criminally insane when I was three years old. My sister is a prostitute, and my father peddles narcotics to school children so he can support his own habit as well as that of his common-law wife.

Recently I met a lovely alcoholic girl was just released from prison where she spent seven years for beating her illegitimate child to death. I would like to marry her.

I want to be honest and open with her so we can start out on the right foot, but I'm afraid of how she might react if I bare my soul.

My question is - should I tell her about my brother who works for Hackers Haven?

DESPERATE AND DESPONDENT

Clarence Klotz
Advice to the woefully inadequate

August 5, 1997

To: DESPERATE AND DESPONDENT

Dear DES,

Yours was one of 437 similar letters received this week and was chosen at random for representative reply. You seem to have three alternatives, each requiring you to bite the bullet a bit.

First, you can just plain not marry the girl, thus not having to share <u>all</u> the degrading aspects of your deranged life.

Second, you can firebomb Hackers Haven, thus at one swoop ridding society of that obvious blemish and nullifying the necessity of revealing to loved ones that a relative works there.

Or, third, you can help your brother prepare an application for employment at Woodfield, the Audy Home or the County Morgue, at the successful conclusion of which you will likewise be relieved of the necessity of confessing to a Hackers Haven connection. Once again out in the sunshine, you can recoup all your emotional losses by writing a book.

Good luck!

Clarence

P.S. Hope this arrives in time to prevent anything drastic. You asked for a prompt reply, and I gave your plea top priority.

Uncle Randy
adviser to the wretched

November 12, 1997

Dear Clarence,

In my business, I am forced to deal with tragedy on a daily basis. As a result, I have become hardened to the point where I can stand back and evaluate the misery and suffering of others without getting personally involved – that is, until I met Gene McDougall.

My heart sank when he slouched into my office. It was obvious that here was a loser if ever there was one. He had not shaved for weeks, and probably not bathed either. His self-image was so negative that it was actually off the charts. Between sobs, he managed to tell me that he, a harmless, elderly man, had been brutalized by one Nelson Campbell. No, he was not clubbed into unconsciousness, nor was he insulted, berated or belittled verbally. Instead, he was subjected to a much more insidious form of abuse. He was mercilessly butchered on the tennis court by this man. It seems that Mr. McDougall had become demoralized after losing most of his matches the past year or two, and in a pathetic attempt to once again experience the thrill of victory, he had jumped at the chance to play an older man – namely, Nelson Campbell. Here, he thought, was his chance to regain some self-respect. But as it turned out, even the age differential was not enough to overcome the skill level gap.

Sir, a man's emotional well-being hangs in the balance. Could you find it in your heart to contact Mr. Campbell (whom I understand you see every day) and see if he would give this poor wretch another chance? Or, failing that, see if Mr. Campbell would send him some flowers or something? I may be clutching at straws, but it seems to me that any gesture of sensitivity and compassion would help.

Concerned, R

Reverend Clarence Klotz

November 16, 1997

Dear Unc,

Last year it was the Mount Prospect Police Department that brought special Christmas cheer and rescued Gene McDougall from the bowels of cynicism. This year let it be a very elder statesman, an Old Man of the Mountain, a Ghost of Christmas Past, so to speak.

I have spoken with Mr. Campbell, and he looks forward to more matches with your client. Meanwhile, Mr. McDougall should despair not. Even though he may see himself in a relative slump, be assured that he is highly regarded by his peers. They rate him a major regional contender in his 70s, a national contender in his 80s and a possible national champion by the time he is 95.

Of course, he may be dealing with a field of two or three in the 95s. He could bye himself into the final. Indeed, the tournament could be played by mail - like chess.

There are hurdles ahead, brother, but his fans, although traditionally quiet, have faith in him. He'll think of something.

Unswervingly yours,

Clarence

Chapter 7
1998

Hypocrites, voice mail, tennis and sex. Names are named.

A vicious band of hypocrites tries to overthrow our duly elected government.

Reverend Elton Jones

February 15, 1998

Dear Clarence,

As brothers of the cloth, I know we both believe in helping those who cannot help themselves. It has come to my attention that one of God's forsaken children needs a kindness done for him. His name is Gene McDougall, and it seems that he recently drove to Hackers Haven Tennis Center only to find that the closest available parking space was fifty feet from the door. Mind you, this man will be 70 years old this year! Is it right that he should be subjected to such a thing? He has led a life that should entitle him to some extra consideration. If he is to be honored while he is still alive, how much longer should we wait? I propose that Hackers Haven immediately put a "Reserved for Gene McDougall" sign in front of the parking space directly in front of the door. Mr. McDougall is entitled to this, as the following will attest:

- He served four years in the Navy, finally achieving the rank of Petty Officer Third Class (the equivalent of Corporal in the Marines). He also spent 2½ years defending Guam, though it must be said that the Japanese had surrendered four years earlier. I personally believe that this was just a timing thing, and not something that should detract from his accomplishment. As if this weren't enough, he is also the proud winner of the coveted Good Conduct Medal.

- His heroism began at an early age. At recess in the fourth grade, he saw a baseball coming down towards the head of one of the other children, so he reached out his hand and deflected the ball so that it fell harmlessly to the ground. Unfortunately, this brave act turned out to have unhappy consequences in that the child he saved later became a lawyer - but at that point in time, who knew?

- About five years ago, he helped a baby duck over a curb so that it could be reunited with its mother and eight siblings who were walking away without it.

Offhand, I cannot think of any other worthwhile thing he has ever done, but I'm sure you will agree that this man certainly deserves a reserved parking space. Can you help?

Thank you and Godspeed,

Elton

Clarence Klotz

February 22, 1998

My dear Brother Elton,

Seventy sounds terribly old all right, but as the crocuses stir and the approaching spring is primed to paint the eager soil, let your friend McDougall despair not. It was Oliver Wendell Holmes who, at 82 and seeing a beautiful girl on a Boston street, sighed, "O to be 70 again!"

Please assure Mr. McDougall that his request for special access to Hackers Haven Tennis Center is under consideration and moving through prescribed channels. This entails referral first to the Sub-Committee on Access Regulations (SCAR), then, pending a positive vote, to the Committee on Overall Policy (COP), then, given another positive vote, to the Committee of the Whole. The club's five permanent employees are well stratified.

You will be kept informed of developments. Meanwhile it has been suggested that Mr. McDougall investigate the possibilities of (a) arriving by motorbike, golf cart or go-kart, thus to end his journey inside the building, or (b) obtaining a physician's statement that might be used in requesting Medicare to pay a portion of the cab fare to and from the club. The latter would allow Mr. McDougall to disembark 30 feet closer to the door than in his stated experience, an apparently crucial distance.

Persevere, old friend. Remember that glorious spring will banish many troubles among us. This inevitable rebirth extends even to Lapland and Lake of the Woods County, Minnesota. As for McDougall, he sounds like a decent sort. Perhaps he is simply bewildered by the ever-changing tides and turns of a world faster than he has ever known. Perhaps a support group...

Clarence

Reverend Elton Jones
Ombudsman for the slow

March 14, 1998

Dear Clarence,

Your advice that Mr. McDougall consider a support group has fallen on deaf ears. When I broached the subject, his only response was that he didn't need any friends – that he had eight television sets. Knowing that he is a dog-lover, I then suggested that he buy a dog for companionship. Although he also dismissed this idea out of hand, I am happy to report that he is considering getting a smaller pet (a slug). In short, we are making progress, although it will take a lot of doing to make him accept the untenable parking situation as it now exists at Hackers Haven.

I showed Mr. McDougall your letter, and he was dismayed to note that you tap-danced around the issue rather than dealing with it head-on. He was especially offended by Hackers Haven's excessively stratified management, which he feels is designed to hinder rather than facilitate progress.

He fears that the logical next step will be voice mail – requiring callers to press a succession of buttons only to find that pressing the last button results in a goodbye message after which the line goes dead. Please - say it is not so!

He also felt that no real effort has been extended to understand his unique situation. For instance, has anyone cared enough to wonder why he never leaves the baseline to approach the net? Obviously, this is too far for him after he has been forced to traverse even greater distances through all kinds of weather just to get from the parking lot to Hackers Haven's door.

Clearly, this drains him of the energy needed to perform optimally when he finally takes the court. A look at his league record will confirm this hypothesis.

I hope the powers-that-be will take another look at this whole matter. Surely an accommodation can be found that would be better than motorbikes, go-carts and Medicare-reimbursed taxi rides. Perhaps you could help set up a task force to do a cost benefit analysis, giving proper credit to the intangible value of the good will which would be generated by a compassionate resolution of this problem.

Sanguinely,

Elton

Clarence Klotz

March 27, 1998

Dear Elton,

Your acquaintance Mr. McDougall is indeed a challenge. What can be done? We hard-working, God-fearing Americans, blessed with almost unlimited resources and a legacy of military and technological successes, tend to feel that no problem is impossible of solution. But are there not some that are, and isn't there a premium on realism, at least in final analysis?

There are times when major problems are beyond our ken, thus I have turned over the burning question "Why doesn't Mr. McDougall take the net?" to a large team of distinguished psychologists. Asked to determine from the data the main reason for this irregularity, they responded as follows:

El Nino	37.8%
Lack of confidence stemming from navy experiences	23.4%
Sun spots	14.3%
Global warming	13.1%
Rejections at Baudette High School	9.8%
No opinion or too overwhelmed by data	1.6%

Please thank Mr. McDougall for his suggestion that voice mail be introduced at his tennis club. Although all the facility's employees are clearly of Rhodes Scholar level, they would never have thought of this. It seems an excellent way to dissipate problems and keep raging members at a distance.

Sympathetically,

Clarence

Jerry Plowwell Service with a smirk
Exorcisms performed, inquisitions financed

April 2, 1998

Dear Clarence,

Our mutual friend, the good reverend Elton Jones, has been involved in a struggle that has become so mean spirited that he finally felt compelled to seek my help, that I might add my considerable weight to God's side of the issue. I speak, of course, of the brouhaha whirling around a proposed reserved parking space at Hacker Haven Tennis Center for Gene McDougall, a worthy, elderly, distinguished and venerable member of the club. I understand that things have now sunk to the point where Hackers Haven has actually threatened to implement a voice mail system in order to discourage contact with its own members. What's worse, in an attempt to put a favorable spin on this vengeful act, Mr. McDougall's words were twisted to make it appear that the voice mail was actually his idea.

Make no mistake, Clarence - when it comes to fighting dirty, I am gloriously equipped to enter the fray. Let us not forget that God speaks to the unwashed masses through me, his loyal and devoted tool here on earth. Those who disagree with me are, by definition, allied with the devil and doomed to an eternity in hell. Something you'd to well to ponder.

Be advised that if a reversal of policy by Hackers Haven is not promptly forthcoming, and the club continues its hateful and immoral attempts to thwart God's will, I will not only perform an exorcism, but will also spend whatever it takes to finance the mother of all inquisitions.

In righteous indignation - your friend,

Jerry

Gene McDougall
loner, misfit, tennis bum

April 30, 1998

Dear Clarence,

I have just learned that a spontaneous widespread outpouring of love and goodwill towards me has resulted in a number of people exerting their influence in a well-meaning but misguided effort to procure a reserved parking space for me at the posh Hackers Haven Tennis Center.

Please understand that I seek no reserved parking space, since I do not feel that the life I have led, though exemplary, is worthy of such an honor. Yes, it is true that I earned the Navy's Good Conduct Medal – yes, I can type 35 words a minute – yes, I conquered my bed-wetting at age 10 – yes, I was graduated 17th in my high school class of 23 souls - the list goes on. Yet I seek no special recognition for my accomplishments, for I am but a simple man who has consistently met each challenge without resorting to the underhanded tactics a lesser person might have employed. For instance, although my tennis game lacks a certain something, I have steadfastly refused to take lessons, having always felt that this would give me an unfair advantage and therefore be tantamount to cheating. Having said this, I must admit to one exception. Several years ago, Jim Merkel did give me some lessons on how to improve my serve. After the lessons were completed, Jim begged me never to tell anyone that they had ever taken place, and to quit telling people that the "Merkel serve" was now a part of my arsenal. Not long thereafter, Jim quit his job at Hackers Haven and, in fact, moved out of the state. Although my telling you this betrays a confidence, I am only a man after all. God has made us imperfect, yet we are created in his image – so what does that say about Him? Sorry. I sometimes digress – a characteristic that is becoming disturbingly more frequent as I slosh through the dung heap of life.

Desultorily,

Gene

Clarence Klotz

May 5, 1998

Friend Elton,

Since you minister to all souls, whatever their rank or station, creed or breed, I hope you will have time between spring revivals to consider the plight of Gene McDougall, a troubled denizen of Arlington Heights, Illinois, about whom we have previously spoken.

His burning issue of the moment is his tennis serve, which has been timed by radar gun at 59, 59, 59. This, while a model of consistency, has been a source of low self-esteem for this wily and otherwise quite successful tournament veteran. Perhaps he would go to the net more if he could be sure that his serve would get there before he does. What can we do, mechanically, mentally or spiritually, for this deserving citizen?

Being a bit more the pragmatist than you, I have a Plan B economic solution in the event your ministrations fall short. It would encourage Gene to take a serving lesson every two weeks, each at a different Chicago-area club. He would use assumed names to avoid possible joint (pro association) hands-off action against him. In all likelihood each teacher would want to divorce himself from any identification with the McDougall serve and be happy to pay him at least $150 for such assurance. Multiply 26 times $150 and you get $3,900, a significant pin-money addition even to the huge retirement payments Gene reportedly receives from his erstwhile employer.

Please keep in touch on this project and assure Mr. McDougall that Jim Merkel did not leave town because of him.

Your devoted colleague,

Clarence

Uncle Randy
advisor to the wretched

May 7, 1998

Dear Clarence,

Your well-meaning but misguided suggestion to Elton Jones that Gene McDougall prostitute himself by blackmailing tennis pros after tricking them into giving him tennis lessons was so sordid that, sad to say, Elton has washed his hands of the whole affair and turned the problem over to me. I have given him my assurance that I would devote my considerable talents to resolving the problem - so, after consulting with my staff as well as outside experts, here are my conclusions:

First, you should know that Elton did not convey your message to Gene McDougall, who is much too honorable a man to hear of such a scheme, let alone take part in such a thing. Gene, therefore, remains blissfully unaware of the controversy raging within the local tennis world regarding his 59 mph serve. By the way, this would be a good time to set the record straight and let you know that this 59 mph serve was recorded more than 10 years ago. The most recent measurement was about five years ago when it was clocked at 49 mph. Should this trend continue, he would eventually be able to beat his serve to the net, a possibility you mentioned in your last letter to Elton. The Catch 22 here is that he runs a little more slowly each year, so the two factors cancel each other out. Ergo, we are still faced with the original problem.

Let us therefore address your question regarding what we can do for him mechanically, mentally or spiritually. For starters, we can throw out "mechanically". If Jim Merkel can ever be found again, I am sure he will attest to the folly of that approach. As for "mentally", no one who has ever met him would consider that to be a viable alternative.

Our only option, then, is to try reaching him "spiritually". We know that nature abhors a vacuum, so it naturally follows that, as an empty vessel, he is susceptible to being filled with whatever enters the void. I propose that you, Elton and I join forces and confront this poor soul with an intervention. Perhaps we can shame him or shock him into relying on a higher power or his own inner strength to overcome his serve - and perhaps some of his other shortcomings as well. A daunting yet noble undertaking, to be sure. Of course, the success of this plan presupposes that we are not too late. If we ARE too late and he has already begun to fill the emptiness of his life with such shallow pleasures as, say, sex, I feel that persuading him to change his priorities would be a hard sell. As mature individuals, we are then left with only one course of action. We must accept the possibility that he could be right, abandon our own value systems and embrace his lifestyle. After all, it seems to be working for him, his pathetic serve notwithstanding. The only downside would be that you and Elton would have to give up God's work and find a job.

Sagely,

Uncle Randy

Gene McDougall
annoying but harmless

May 14, 1998

Open letter to all the ladies I have known:

You are wonderful. Having said that, I have noticed one teensy little imperfection that seems to be common to all members of your species, and it involves verbal communications. The problem as well as the solution is presented in the following work, hereinafter to be known as:

The McDougall Theorem

- If you speak to a man, you cannot expect that he will hear and/or understand your message if you are farther away from him than some other noise such as running water, TV, radio or microwave. The louder the interfering noise, the closer you must be to the man if he is to hear you. The mid-point is reached when your distance from him and the distance of the competing noise are equidistant after factoring in the decibel level of both inputs. At that point, the man will be able to hear both noises, but the voice will sound like gibberish.

- The same problem exists if there is no competing noise, but you are facing away from the man as you speak. Again, decibels play a role here, but a soft-spoken woman will not be able to overcome the fact that her sound waves are travelling AWAY from the man.

There it is - "The McDougall Theorem" - brilliant in its simplicity, yet absolutely essential if heterosexual relationships are to survive and flourish. I offer this to the world because life has been good to me, and I just want to give something back. I seek no monetary reward, but to those of you who are nevertheless moved to send donations, please send cash only – no checks. If you send $100 or more, I will present you with your very own autographed copy of the "McDougall Theorem," suitable for framing.

Best wishes,

Gene

CLARENCE KLOTZ
Cleric-Philosopher-Confidant
Hands held • Problems studied • Riots managed

June 3, 1998

Dear Uncle Randy,

As a court of last resort, you indeed have some seemingly impossible disciples/patients. Reaching this man McDougall spiritually appears one of the toughest assignments of our time. If you can turn him around, you'll deserve a picnic.

How does one get a job like yours?

The McDougall Theorem is, well, every bit as earthshaking as any of his previous axioms. While it doesn't rank with Newton's Laws, or even Murphy's, it does harken us back to simpler days. It reminds this old campaigner of his son's profound initial reaction to elementary school study of Pavlov's Response, "If you mistreat your dog, he'll bite you." Who can argue with the thesis that the closer you are to a person, the more chance you'll have of hearing him?!

And he may be right, that even I, a man of boundless energy to serve humanity, should junk it and get a job.

Pensively,

Clarence

cc:
Albert Schweitzer Foundation
American Psychological Association
Ann Landers

Uncle Randy
advisor to the wretched

June 15, 1998

Dear Clarence,

Our mutual friend, Gene McDougall, has gotten himself into one sweet pickle this time. He has had the temerity to write an inflammatory letter to the Daily Herald (see enclosure), and now he fears for his safety. He has requested that you, as a God-fearing man he knows and trusts, hold this letter for safekeeping and turn it over to the authorities if anything untoward happens to him – like, say, if he is murdered gangland style.

As you can see, his letter turns over some rocks, and God knows what evil will crawl out from under them. Had he sought my counsel before this impetuous act, I would have advised him to continue the low profile existence that has kept him alive and well for almost 70 years – but as you know, he is not easily dissuaded when he sees a chance to expose an injustice or right a wrong.

God bless and protect this wonderful man,

Uncle Randy

Gene McDougall
retired

June 15, 1998

LETTER TO THE EDITOR

Three years ago a plan to widen Kensington Road from two to three lanes was shoved down our throats. As of today, June 15, here are the results:

The stop light added at Kensington and West Regency Drive West (at the high school entrance) is causing traffic backups on Kensington, something that never occurred before. This means that our tax dollars have been squandered to solve a problem that never existed until the "solution" was implemented. Since Kensington traffic is about ten times that of the intersecting Regency Drive West traffic, why is the green light <u>shorter</u> for Kensington than for the less used street? If a sensor is involved, it is not working.

The new Kensington Road is several inches lower than the original. This makes the grading of the wheelchair ramps illegal (too steep). To bring these ramps into compliance will take up to 48 feet of grading per ramp.

The new lines painted on Regency Drive West have created three lanes where there were two before. One problem - these lanes are now too narrow to meet government requirements. Dozens of new trees have recently been planted along Kensington, almost directly under the power and phone lines. Does the word "nitwit" ring a bell? The village, the state and ComEd all agree that most power outages are caused by tree limbs. Trees – limbs – get the connection? Hello?

Who is benefiting from all this? If you think this is something the Illinois Attorney General should look into, clip out this letter and send it to him along with your own comments. Don't bother writing to the mayor or the village board members. I did this when there was still time to stop all this – and not one of them had the decency to reply.

Gene McDougall

Uncle Randy
advisor to the wretched

July 2, 1998

Dear Clarence,

Emboldened by the fact that no violence upon his person or property occurred after his recent "letter to the editor" attacking the local political scoundrels, Gene McDougall (against my advice) has written another provocative letter (see enclosure).

He seems way too in touch with his inner child, yet one must admire his passionate lifelong battle against evil – often at great cost to his own well being. I have explained to him that after just so many such letters, people will begin to think of him as a crackpot and dismiss his message out of hand. He reacts to such advice by staring at me, slowly walking away or sometimes just giggling. Disquieting, I'm sure you would agree.

Since I seem unable to reach him, I am begging for your help. As a man of the cloth, perhaps you can connect with him at another level (logic hasn't worked). It's a long shot, but I don't know where else to turn. Can you help?

Desperately,

Uncle Randy

Gene McDougall
retired

July 2, 1998

LETTER TO THE EDITOR

During WWII, the street signs in many European cities were removed to confuse enemy troop movements, should they be invaded. Last month, right here in America, the street sign at the intersection of Regency Drive West and Kensington Road in Arlington Heights was removed when the new traffic lights were installed.

I am frightened.

Do the Arlington Heights authorities know something we don't? Is an invasion imminent? If Canadian troops are massing at the border, we should be told. If not, we should have the street sign restored.

It is important that ComEd, the phone company, the police and the fire department and others get here quickly when needed, but now that the street sign is gone, some of our service providers have been unable to find our neighborhood until after they have called back for additional directions. At the present time, the simplest way to direct them here is to tell them to go east on Kensington Road and turn left on the street with no name at the improperly calibrated traffic light by the school.

God help us all.

Gene McDougall

Clarence Klotz

July 15, 1998

Dear Unc,

Your man McDougall is perhaps needlessly apprehensive about his survival. The time-honored Klotz Kanon holds that the risk to an activist citizen's well-being varies inversely with the strength of his profile. In short, the little guys are likely to get it before the big guys. The maxim clearly failed in the cases of Gandhi and King, but the odds are with McDougall.

Who among us would harm a folk hero who, after one more epic letter, may be seeded alongside Paine, Zola, Tolstoy and Voltaire. You can fight city hall, brother.

Encourage your disciple to hang in there. He seems a little unusual, but when one's heart is in the right place, who are we to criticize?

Empathetically,

Clarence

The venerable Reverend Elton Jones

July 31, 1998

Dear Clarence,

For decades, "separate but equal accommodations" has been the rallying cry of segregationists. In actual practice, however, separate accommodations have never been equal – nor can they be. Case in point – the proposed upgrading of the women's locker room at the Hackers Haven Tennis Center. I presume that up to now the men's locker room has been superior to the women's. With the new plan, it is obvious that the ladies' locker room will now have the most square footage and the more modern fixtures. This example should convince you that separate but equal is an impossible dream. Throughout the years, maintaining two locker rooms has cost Hackers Haven untold thousands of dollars more than it would have cost to maintain just one unisex facility. Please use your influence with Hackers Haven's management to integrate these locker and shower facilities. Synergy can be a powerful thing, as the recent merger-mania among our largest corporations will attest. Here are but a few of the benefits which would accrue to the Club and its membership:

- The long-standing hostility between the men and women of Hackers Haven, fueled by perceived locker room inequities, would finally end.

- Both sexes would benefit from a more friendly and informal inter-relationship. A happy club is a successful club.

- The chances of romances blossoming between members would increase by leaps and bounds.

- Granted, the membership rolls might shrink somewhat as the more reserved females drop out. But hey – who needs those bluenoses anyhow?

Time is on our side. This is the wave of the future. We must choose to be in the vanguard of enlightened change. Otherwise, we will be hauled kicking and screaming into the twenty-first century. Progress cannot be stopped. Be bold - grab the ring and hop on.

I believe I was born for this crusade. If I am remembered for one thing, I pray it will be this gift I offer to all those who yearn for a better, happier world of peace and harmony.

Fervently,

Elton

Renovating Hackers Haven

Clarence Klotz

August 4, 1998

To: The venerable Reverend Elton Jones

Dear Ven,

For us Little Picture folks, it's always a tonic to commune with those of you who see the Big Picture. Who but a tiny intellectual segment of the world's teeming billions could see a tennis club's renovation program as part of one of society's gnawing social problems?

Your unisex locker room proposal might, by extension, be transferred to other walks of confrontational life. For example, one of my disciples has a Golden Rule-based plan to bring into mutual understanding such disparate groups as:

- The Ku Klux Klan and the Black Panthers
- The Mossad and the Hezbollah
- The Union League Club and Hell's Angels
- The Christian Coalition and Agnostics Anonymous
- The Hitler Youth and the Young Communist League

You get the idea. Do you think Golden Rule leaflets and conscience-raising sessions will be enough?

On the more mundane local scene, please understand that even after expansion, the women's locker room at Hackers Haven will be considerably smaller than the men's. Even after expansion, the man's lockers will outnumber the women's, 70-54, with more than half the latter being half-lockers. The world may not be ready for a Reverend Jones foray into the current women's locker room, but such an inspection may be arranged. Those quarters have been unaffectionately characterized by even well-wishers as "crackerbox," "sardine can" and/or "phone booth." While I have been part of the management scene since 1971 and admit to numerous mistakes in a misspent life, I can prove that I had no part in the original women's locker room design. Thank goodness. Keep them cards 'n letters comin'. Your ideas are ever welcome, stimulating and reflective of the ingenuity and vibrance that has made America great, even if they don't get used.

Affectionately,

Clarence

Maury Lifschitz attorney at law
"NO CASE TOO FRIVOLOUS"

September 8, 1998

Dear Mr. Klotz,

As an ambitious trial attorney, my mouth waters as I look at the document I have in front of me. It tells me that you have not only committed plagiarism, but you have compounded the offense by sending the material through the U. S. Mail. Your attempt to smear my client by clipping a right-wing article out of the paper and pasting his name over the real author's name is serious business and cannot be ignored.

You may wonder how this crime was so quickly and easily traced to you. Well, my friend, you simply underestimated your victim. Mr. McDougall recognized your M.O. as soon as the envelope arrived addressed in crayon and with no return address. The letter itself was typed, and matched previous letters known to have come from your typewriter. This will give you some idea of how formidable an adversary you face. Mr. McDougall and I agree that this is our big chance to get rich, since we know you have deep pockets. Not only are you a large investor in the Hackers Haven Tennis Center, a local enterprise known to be a cash cow, but you have authored several books, which everyone knows is a great way to make easy money. As if that weren't enough, it is common knowledge that you have won money in tennis tournaments. God only knows what other sources of revenue you enjoy. Bottom line - you can save yourself a lot of money and agony if we can agree on a settlement before this case ever gets to court. You are invited to call our law offices within the next few days to set up an appointment.

Litigiously,

Maury

EARL "SHIFTY" GEARS
Attorney at Law
Ambulance chasing • Bankruptcy counsel
Appraisals (high or low/depending)

September 10, 1998

Dear Mr. Lifchitz,

In response to your letter of September 8 re the alleged dangerous criminal Clarence Klotz, I submit two positions, to be studied in advance of any appointment.

First, re evidence if any, my client deposes (a) that he has never met or seen the author of the alleged article, (b) that he has plagiarized nothing, (c) that he always wears gloves when he types letters, (d) that Smith Corona sold 534,289 typewriters of his model last year and (e) that even dropouts among us recognize the similarity between the prose at issue and the work of the modern H. L. Mencken, Gene McDougall. Normally a God-fearing, humble, congenial man, my client takes refuge in a profundity made famous by such distinguished statesmen as Tony Accardo, Jimmy Hoffa and Willie Sutton: "Youse can't prove nuthin."

Second, re financial condition, my client submits the following report, not likely to encourage angle-shooters:

>   Total money won in tennis..................$25.00
>   Total profit from book sales.....................0.00
>   Surplus funds. Hackers Haven holdings......0.00
>   Total such funds available for litigation ...$25.00

Given these figures, your one-third share in the unlikely event of a successful suit would be $8.33.

Yours for greener pastures,

Earl

Maury Lifschitz attorney at law
"NO CASE TOO FRIVOLOUS"

September 15, 1998

Dear Mr. Gears,

Your letter defending the actions of your client, Clarence Klotz, did not move me. However, when you provided the details of his financial condition, I began to do some number crunching and finally decided to let your client off the hook. I must admit that the $8.33 profit potential you mentioned was a major turn-off. I can only hope that we put a scare into your client, so that he will now mend his ways. After all, that's what we're here for – to make the world a better place, one person at a time.

I'm sure I could have somehow tied the cross-plagiarism to his private sex life, thereby exposing him to the possibility of life imprisonment or lethal injection – or at the very least, public humiliation (or envy). But frankly, I do not have the expertise to successfully conceive and execute the invasion of privacy and entrapment which would be required. Such tactics are best left to professional hit-men such as Ken Starr and his ilk.

In short, Mr. Gears, I have decided to take the high road and drop this entire matter. But as brothers before the bar, you may be interested in joining me in a plan which could more than compensate us for the time and effort we have already spent on this matter. I propose that we tell our respective clients that we are negotiating an out-of-court settlement, and then after two or three years, announce that the case has been dropped in the best interests of both parties.

Alas, that means no one-third cut for me, but the amount of money we could each collect by billing our clients for three or four hours a week over a period of several years could easily pay for a well-deserved vacation in the Caymans for both of us. It goes without saying that we would go at the same time, meet with each other, discuss the case and then write the whole thing off.

Please advise,

Maury

Lifschitz

CLARENCE KLOTZ
Friend to the friendless

October 1, 1998

Dear Elton,

Trading cosmic observations with you or your fiduciary, Maury "No Case Too Frivolous" Lifschitz, is indeed one of the rewards of life. The latter's September 15 letter to "Shifty" Gears struck many tender chords.

If I had $42,000 a day in the bag, the promise of unlimited funds from a big daddy if needed, three years in which to work and the luxury of illegal phone recordings provided by a disgruntled ex-employee out to write a tell-all book, I could embarrass even such beloved personages as

>   Abe Lincoln
>   Albert Schweitzer
>   St. Francis of Assisi
>   Florence Nightingale
>   Gene McDougall

In a similar vein, expecting mortals to tell the truth about their sex lives is naïveté indeed. Who ever does? It has been my unscientific observation that 40 percent of the people say they're having more than they are. These are the boasters. Another 40 percent say they're having less than they are. These are the predators. That leaves 20 percent, the in-betweens. For one reason or another, they'll lie, too, if the dreaded subject ever comes up.

So much for high thinking. Share your views when the spirit moves you. Meanwhile, Mr. Gears looks forward to sojourning with Mr. Lifschitz in the Caymans. He banks there.

Loyally,

Clarence

Reverend Elton Jones
goodness incarnate

October 2, 1998

Dear Clarence,

Your letter of yesterday warmed the cockles of my heart (cold cockles are a bummer). To continue on the subject of Salem revisited, I thought you might enjoy this excerpt from the Dilbert Newsletter:

"Some Induhviduals (sic) say it's not the sex, it's the lying that's the real problem. But it's not a general kind of lying that's the problem, it's specifically the President's unwillingness to share details of his sex life with every human being in the world. By that standard, only Geraldo Rivera and Dennis Rodman could qualify to be President."

I know we feel powerless in a world controlled by evil, but there is one small blow we can strike for mankind. VOTE! And get everyone in your congregation to vote, as I plan to do. When the evildoers are cast from the House (and the Senate), what a day that will be. We can then triumphantly watch Gingrich, Falwell, Starr, Reed, Buchanan, Robertson, Helms, et al. begin their inevitable slide into the cesspool of history. The sheer joy of it sets me to quivering. Glory be!

Rejoice – November 3, the day of judgement, is near.

Ecstatically,

Elton

Clarence Klotz

November 12, 1998

Dear Elton,

Your friends had no idea you wielded so much national influence. You exhorted our citizens to vote, and they did!

Gingrich is certainly a great loss to America. How often are we blessed in high places with a shakedown artist who misapplies the proceeds, a "family values" man who has apparently had numerous affairs while married, a hawk/patriot who avoided service by marrying an older teacher whom he divorced in part because "she wasn't attractive enough to be a First Lady" and a man who continually and pompously misjudges the pulse of the people.

The Democrats must hate to see him go, at least for a while. They lose an easy target, and who wouldn't want to play against a shortstop who makes five errors a game?

Meanwhile the humility you have displayed in the wake of your towering tennis victory over the indomitable Ken Schaller has entranced us all. Despite the natural acclaim accruing from such a feat, you remain the same unassuming, down-to-earth person we've always known.

Collegially,

Clarence

The venerable Reverend Elton Jones
On the run somewhere in Europe

November 16, 1998

Dear Clarence,

In my zeal to make the world a better place, I may have acted rashly. I recently e-mailed a message to Charles Grodin of MSNBC TV, which, if my identity as the author becomes known, will make me a marked man. Here is the letter:

"Dear Mr. Grodin,

I think I have found a way to neutralize two of the most dangerous sociopaths among us in one fell swoop, the details of which I hereby submit for your consideration:

1. Terminate Ken Starr's unseemly attempts to overthrow our government and instead authorize him to conduct an open-ended, lifelong investigation of O. J. (Orenthal) Simpson. I'm sure the costs associated with such an endeavor could easily be covered by public donations.

2. Starr's first act should be to prosecute Orenthal for his perjury in the civil trial during which he swore under oath that he did not kill his wife and Ron Goldman. Why these charges have never been brought mystifies and depresses me.

3. Starr's next step should be to subpoena hundreds of people, if need be, in order to uncover every detail of Orenthal's past and present sex life which is no doubt rife with indictable offenses. For instance, I have seen him on videotape boasting that the first time he had sex with Nicole, he raped her. Tenaciously pursuing this avenue of the investigation would be a special perk for Starr, who so obviously finds this type of thing stimulating and gratifying.

4. Since Orenthal is a known murderer, it is entirely logical to assume he has killed before. Ken Starr would be the perfect one to delve into every unsolved murder that ever occurred within 50 miles of Orenthal from the time he was 14 to the present day. With the new investigative techniques now available – including DNA – this could yield spectacular results and, at the very least, keep Orenthal engaged in costly litigation for the rest of his life. This might very well elevate Starr's public image from "scum of the earth" to just plain "asshole."

If you choose to use this letter on your program, please do not use my name. I am a physical coward and deathly afraid of offending either of those two predators."

Well Clarence, there it is.

Pray for me,

Elton

Clarence Klotz

November 25, 1998

Dear Brother Elton,

It was only a matter of time before a habitue of Warsaw USA (or his agent) would journey to the original Warsaw. If Mr. Grodin is not impressed with the suggestions and/or sentiments contained in your letter from that capital, this old campaigner is.

With your permission I shall use a copy of said letter as part of a document nominating Kenneth Starr for Asshole of the Year, an award approaching stature equal to Time's Man of the Year. In the event you have not heard of this competition, consider the list of past winners:

> Newt Gingrich
> John McEnroe
> Bob Knight
> Slobodan Milosevic
> Ilie Nastase
> Ex-Gov. Mechem of Arizona

As you might guess, the competition is fierce. This is best demonstrated by the revelation that Dick Armey, Jesse Helms, Billy Packer and Pat Buchanan have so far been mere also-rans. Rush Limbaugh came closest to the tin ring, but his best year was Gingrich's. When it comes to assholes, who could ever deny Newt?

Diogenes himself would have a hard time finding citizens who would tell the truth about sex. Thomas Jefferson didn't. Chances are that some of the Kinsey Report respondents didn't either, even though guaranteed anonymity.

Empathetically,

Clarence

Reverend Elton Jones
Somewhere in Russia

December 11, 1998

Dear Clarence,

Charles Grodin chose not to use my November 16 e-mail suggesting that Ken Starr turn his attention from Bill Clinton to Orenthal Simpson. Therefore, the heat is off. I now feel it is safe for me to return to the United States in the near future.

But before that, since the season of peace and love is almost upon us, I would like to respond to your excellent November 25 list of evil people with a list of my own. My list, in keeping with the spirit of Christmas, is in praise of the heroes who have graced our world during the 20th century:

Winston Churchill – who kept Hitler at bay all alone for two years with nothing more than his inspirational words as weapons.

Edward R. Murrow – who finally attacked Joe McCarthy publicly. Something that even presidents, to their everlasting shame, had not found the courage to do.

Joseph Welch – the attorney who represented the Army in the Army-McCarthy hearings, and in the process, exposed McCarthy as the despicable demogogue that he was.

Larry Flynt – Who helped preserve free speech in our country by winning his Supreme Court case against Jerry Falwell, and more recently offering rewards for information about the sexual misdeeds of the members of Congress who are so eager to judge our president. I understand the responses are pouring in. Bravo, Larry!

Nelson Campbell – who has always unflinchingly given of his time and effort to counsel those in need. I refer specifically to such needy souls as Maury Lifschitz, Earl "Shifty" Gears, Rod Everhard, Uncle Randy, Gene McDougall, Billy Bob "Hoss" Gonzales, Montmorency J. Tillingast, H. J. Hallstrom, Hortense Snavely, Reginald Q. Twillingham, J. P. Kennedy Rockefeller, Terrance "Bulldog" Twitherspoon, et al.

We can only hope that the good people of the world will ultimately prevail even though it is hard for the weak amongst us to keep the faith when they can see that the bad people keep killing the good people. In spite of this, I tenaciously cling to the notion that in the end all will be well.

Sanguinely,

Elton

Reverend Elton Jones

December 28, 1998

Dear Clarence,

Always searching for ways to make the world a better place, I have decided to share some driving tips with the multitude of lesser beings out there who are not as gifted as I am behind the wheel of an automobile:

When making a right turn into an intersection, make a large swing into the next lane so you will enter the intersecting street head-on instead of at an angle. This will keep your right rear tire from going over the curb. When turning left, you can forego the swing-out and instead just enter the street at a severe angle, slicing through the lane meant for the intersecting street's oncoming traffic. This sometimes gets a little messy collision-wise because of the frightful number of drivers out there who do not drive defensively.

By the way, both of the above maneuvers usually get me noticed, causing an enthusiastic response to my bumper sticker, "Honk if you love Jesus." In the summer, when car windows are open, I can even hear other drivers calling out His name.

Speeders are always a concern. You can do your part to slow them down by using your turn signals even when you have no plans to turn. This will confuse most drivers, causing many of them to slow down. I usually drive five or ten miles per hour under the posted limit. One simply cannot be too careful. You'd be surprised at how many accidents I see all around me every day.

You have my cell phone number. Call me any time. Always glad to chat. It gives me something to do while driving.

Happy motoring,

Elton

Chapter 8
1999

More names are named, causing the writer to go underground. And a revolutionary chromosome-based solution to the nation's high crime rate is unveiled.

By blending in with the crowd, Elton hopes to keep a low profile.

CLARENCE KLOTZ
Friend to Those Who Have No Friends*

January 14, 1999

Dear Elton,

Your December 11 letter from the Old Country was indeed received. We septuagenarians have difficulty estimating the passage of time. In casual conversation we sometimes overestimate, sometimes underestimate. It's hell to get old.

Forgetfulness is another of our shortcomings. I apologize profusely for failing to award even honorable mention to Jerry Falwell, Pat Robertson and Congressman Bob Barr on the All-Asshole squad. The assemblage looks weak without them. If he is still alive, Lester "Ax Handle" Maddox also deserves first-team consideration. Or even if he isn't.

Please give Barr every opportunity to shine. He has great credentials. He spoke before a bunch of Kluxers, championed some of their views, then later claimed he didn't know those views in advance. That had to be a lie. Too, this paragon of Congressional virtue is up on a paternity or child support rap. He could be a starter on the Assholes, not just a bench warmer.

Yesterday I received a postcard from Novgorod, Russia — in an envelope because the postal folk wouldn't accept cards. Delivery time: 26 days.

Keep the faith,

Clarence

---

* with apologies to Boston Blackie, who may have been before your time.

Reverend Elton Jones

January 21, 1999

Dear Clarence,

I'm embarrassed. Your letter of January 14 correctly pointed out a grave error on my part. Obviously, Bob Barr, whom I left off my list of famous people from Georgia, clearly has earned his right to occupy a special place on that list (as well as in Hell). That I failed to include him can only be attributed to building my list while so enraged that I became temporarily incapable of the calm deliberation needed to do the job properly. Had I not allowed my righteous indignation to control my behavior, I would have taken the time to do my research more thoroughly.

While I agree with your opinion that Jimmy Carter is a good man, much depends upon what the word "good" means. To many, "good" is considered the opposite of "evil." On the other hand, the phrase, "You done good" suggests that "good" can also be used to describe a level of competence. If you will review my January 8 letter, you will see that my list was made up of famous people from Georgia. The key word here is "famous," and it should be noted that I offered no further characterizations (good, evil or incompetent).

And finally, in the spirit of love and reconciliation, I would like to come to the defense of the Republicans who have been so viciously assailed for ignoring the will of the people. In all fairness, we should recognize that they are not accountable to the American people at large, but only to their own constituents. As we know, those constituents are Big Tobacco, the National Rifle Association, the Christian Coalition and other white supremacist and hate groups.

I invite you to join me in the comforting thought that all is well in this, the best of all possible worlds.

Blissfully,

Elton

CLARENCE KLOTZ
Confessor, Confidant, Ally, Friend

February 1, 1999

Dear Brother Elton,

As in all walks of life, there is a continuing need to develop new blood, persons to carry the ball when the established veterans begin to lose effectiveness.

So it is with assholes. Gingrich, Knight, Robertson and McEnroe won't last forever, and if the word they represent is to have any long-term meaning, there must be a youth movement. In this vein I nominate Ollie North and Ralph Reed. Each shows great promise, yet each needs a little more seasoning at the major league level. You may be surprised that Dan Quayle failed to make the cut. It was the position of the committee that he is simply too dumb. To be an effective asshole, one needs an IQ of at least 120, a spokesperson declared, and none of the members felt Quayle could come close to that figure.

Now there are charlatans and con artists among us, brother, thus an opinion survey re North and Reed to which I invite your participation. Reid may be sincere in his positions, yet be a national danger just the same. North may have served with distinction as a Marine under fire, yet as you and I know so well, there is no shortage of assholes in the armed forces. Check below the expression that most closely represents your sentiments re North and Reed:

- They're sincere. They believe their positions are right, moral, patriotic and necessary.

- They may believe some of their stuff, but primarily they're con artists who've found a way to grab headlines, curry favor with certain segments of society and make money.

- They're simply extreme conservative politicians who have wrapped themselves in the flag and/or the Lord as a means of achieving legitimacy.

America needs assholes. What would cartoonists do without them? How much less conversational material would there be in the bars and barber shops of such urban centers as Baudette, Minnesota. and Coal City, Illinois? What price excitement?

Looking forward to your continued input, I remain

Earnestly,

Clarence

P.S. I have received a nice card from Tomsk, Siberia. It was only 10 days in transit. Wasn't there a verse about a guy from Omsk who met a guy from Tomsk?

February 15, 1999
THE FOXHUNT

Once upon a time, there was a fox who noticed some chickens living in (you guessed it) a chicken shack, so Mr. Fox decided to pay them a visit. After all, who doesn't like chicken? But as luck would have it, some evil men had been waiting in the shadows for his arrival, and they swooped down upon him and took him prisoner.

As Mr. Fox watched and listened from his cage, the ugly truth became clear. He was to be the object of a (gasp) foxhunt. As Mr. Fox well knew, this "sport" consists of a dozen hounds and another dozen or so gallant men on horseback romping through the countryside chasing a fox until he (or she) is cornered. When the hapless fox realizes escape is impossible, he rolls over on his back (the time-honored signal of submission), desperately hoping for mercy. But alas, it is not to be, since the hounds are trained to tear the exhausted, frightened and defenseless fox to pieces. The sight of this bloody feeding frenzy delights the noble horsemen, who then spend the rest of the day congratulating each other and celebrating their heroic victory.

Knowing all this, Mr. Fox was filled with trepidation as he saw the hunting party approaching his cage, for he knew this meant that the dreaded day had come. It was apparent that the largest of the advancing horsemen was the man in charge. "Perhaps," thought Mr. Fox, "I can beg this man for mercy, for after all, aren't fat folks supposed to be jolly and easy-going?"

But first impressions can be deceiving. Mr. Fox's blood ran cold when the gluttonous one spoke in a voice trembling with hate, "Well, Mr. Fox, now we are going to make you sorry you were ever born. How do you like that?"

"But why, sir, do you want to do me such grievous harm?" asked Mr. Fox plaintively.

"Because," droned the corpulent one, "you are a chicken-killer. I'm doing this for the chickens."

"But," implored Mr. Fox, "haven't you yourself killed chickens?"

"We can't compare your actions to mine, Mr. Fox," the grotesquely obese one replied indignantly, "because mine was a youthful indiscretion, whereas yours were, well, done by you."

"With all due respect," observed Mr. Fox, "am I not, in fox years, about the same age you were when you did your 'youthful' dirty deed? And don't you realize that the decent people in the village will recoil in horror at the savagery you plan to unleash upon me?"

"It is not up to me," the rotund one replied as a string of saliva oozed from the edge of his mouth and slowly rolled down his chin where it dangled precariously like a quivering icicle, "Big fish eat little fish and animals eat each other to survive. You see, it's nature's law, and I am simply doing what I must - following the rule of law."

At this point, the huge one's horse, no longer able to bear its heavy burden, collapsed – sending the round one rolling like a giant pumpkin down a hill and out of sight, never to be seen again. Without the blubbery one to spur the hunters on, interest quickly faded, Mr. Fox was freed, the villagers rejoiced and everyone lived happily ever after. *

* The happy ending is for the kids. Real-life outcomes may vary.

CLARENCE KLOTZ
Confessor, Confidant, Ally, Friend

February 20, 1999

Dear Brother Elton,

Your "Foxhunt" allegory is excellent. It hits the issue squarely, places the tormentors in a light they truly deserve and should remind even the author's severest critics that he is a literary force to be reckoned with. (There is yet time!)

Why is it that allegories, cartoons and ballads can wake up a populace when mere words can't?

In your glee do not succumb to overconfidence. The Fat One may seem dead, but remember Richard Nixon and the fact that the Republicans really have nobody at the moment.

Meanwhile, keep on writin'.

Collegially,

Clarence

Reverend Elton Jones

March 10, 1999

Dear Clarence,

Each day becomes more precious in inverse proportion to how many of them we have left. As one old fart to another, I have decided to share some of my secrets for eliminating those activities that rob us of what little time remains.

First of all, I have given up reading fiction. This would include most novels. Hell, none of that stuff is even true, for God's sake!

Shaving is futile. I have never yet shaved without all the hair growing right back. Screw it.

Bathing seems to be nothing more than a foolish ritual. Dirt immediately begins to re-accumulate, so what's the point? In a month or two, you're as dirty as before. God has provided us with a more healthy and natural way of washing away impurities – sweat. At least once a week, I exercise vigorously and that does the trick. It is comforting to know that God provides solutions for everything. For instance, fish never bathe, but they do not need to because God, in his infinite wisdom, has seen to it that they are constantly immersed in water. Just part of his great plan. If God wanted us to be immersed in water, even part of the time, we would have fins.

Brushing my teeth, like shaving and bathing, seems to be a pointless, time-consuming activity. And it is certainly not natural. If it were, we would pick up the habit on our own rather than be forced into it by our parents. True, one's teeth will fall out earlier than would otherwise have been the case, so the total time previously saved by not brushing could later be squandered trying to do such things as gumming corn on the cob - but note that I said, "could be." To get around this, simply switch to creamed corn – and substitute applesauce for apples, carrot juice for carrots and so on. One might even consider baby food. Sure, false teeth are a possibility, but I do not consider that to be a viable option because taking them in and out of your mouth every day, as well as cleaning them over and over again, probably would take more time than brushing the original ones would have taken in the first place.

I try to keep conversations with other people to an absolute minimum. Interacting with others requires the observance of a great many unpleasant and hard-to-master rules (real or feigned interest in the problems of others, courtesy, rage control and, in my case at least, being thick-skinned enough to allow personal insults to roll like water off a duck's back). I have partially solved this problem by staying home except for rare trips to the grocery store (for food) and the tennis club (for sweating).

And finally, sex seems to be rather pointless. True, it only takes two or three minutes, but it's messy and what has been accomplished? You end up right where you were before you started – except more tired. And you will never get those two or three minutes back.

By incorporating these tips into your daily life, you will free up countless hours to be better spent enjoying all the beautiful things in life – none of which spring immediately to mind.

I hope this has been helpful,

Elton

Reverend Elton Jones

March 14, 1999

Dear Clarence,

As I sit here in solitary gloom listening to my arteries harden and my body deteriorate, an overpowering feeling of despair engulfs me. Do I have time left to turn my life into something that will allow me to die a happy and fulfilled man?

I think so.

Little by little, my unrealized dreams, missed opportunities and outright failures have provided me with a wealth of experience to draw upon as I put together my exciting new business plan. This time, I have a winner if there ever was one. Forget the door-to-door breast exam service, the mom and pop fire station – forget all the traditional thinking that has held me back in the past. I have transcended all that and am now thinking outside the box. Hold on to your hat. Are you ready? I intend to form a not-for-profit religious organization! Ninety percent of the money taken in will be paid to me in salary and bonuses, with 10% going to the various charities that we will support. Do you see the beauty in this? The Elton Jones Charity Foundation (EJCF) will need to do no heavy lifting, as it were (no hands-on work among the poor, the diseased or the otherwise distasteful). All EJCF need do is select which charities to donate 10 percent of our income to, and feather our nest with what is left.

I would not have told you all this if I could not find a way for you to share in the profits. I am pleased at this time to offer you the position of Chief Charity Selector (CCS) of EJCF. You will be in charge of the entire 10% of total EJCF income earmarked for charity, with the responsibility of choosing which charities are selected to receive our money.

Half of this amount goes into your pocket as compensation for your services. At first glance, this may not seem like much, but don't forget that we haven't factored in the kickbacks to you from the charities vying for our handouts. Make no mistake – we're talking big money here, brother!

And here's the grabber. As men of the cloth running a not-for-profit organization, we will never pay a dime in taxes! Is this a great country or what? To seal the deal, I am prepared to offer you the other half of your 10% budget to run the media operation necessary to produce our income. After some number crunching, this appears to leave nothing for the charities, but we can work that out later. The important thing is to get started ASAFP.

Praise the Lord,

Elton

Clarence Klotz

March 16, 1999

Dear Colleague Elton,

Once again I revel in your creativity and the opportunity to participate in one of your legendary projects. O, that everyone could be a CCS of EJCF a thus feel that rush of accomplishment normally accruing to a CEO, ADM or MVP.

Naturally I am mulling over lists upon lists of potential charities for our work. Following are the leaders so far:

- The Nelson Campbell Foundation

- Save the Whippoorwills

- Golfers Anonymous (support group in national interest; if you feel a temptation to play, call a fellow member and he'll talk you out of it)

- Abigail Cabot's School for Wayward Girls

- The O'Flaherty College of Technology (school motto: "Education Is Good")

- The Committee to Abolish Professional Boxing

- Citizens for the Abolition of Disco Music in America (CADMA)

- Committee to Impeach Juan Antonio Samaranch (CIJAS)

- Equal Rights for Dropouts

- National Hospital for Moonshiner Rehabilitation

- Drag Racers' Hall of Fame

- Speech Therapy USA (designed to rid vocabularies of "ya know?" and "ya know what I mean?")

- Dennis Rodman Charm School

- Bikers for Shakespeare

- Thrusts for Peace (bringing together gentler elements of the KKK, Jihad, IRA, El Rukns and Serb militias)

- Mike Tyson Chair for the Study of Intergender Relationships

There you have a glorious Sweet Sixteen. While they are not in exact order of preference, you will understand why No. 1 must remain No.1. Given your generous financial breakdown, I come up with the following hypothetical situation based on an initial fund-raising of $5,000:

You get $4,500, leaving $500 for my end of the bargain. Of the $500, half is mine, and half goes toward the work. Of the latter $250, you say half is discretionary (heh-heh!), leaving $125 for actual charity. Dividing $125 by 15, the number of non-Campbell beneficiaries, we get $8.33 for each. Not overwhelming, some may say, but it's income beyond budget. What kick will they have?

Please keep me informed of project details.

Compatriotically,

Clarence

Reverend Elton Jones

March 20, 1999

Dear Clarence,

I was pleased to see the alacrity with which you accepted your new position as CCF of EJCF. Obviously, you have the vision to see the possibilities for wealth beyond measure if we manage the operation properly.

It was heart-warming to see that, in just a few days, you had zealously compiled a list of 16 charities to consider. In that regard, may I be so bold as to make one teensy suggestion? Instead of giving all 16 of them an equal portion of the contributions, you might wish to consider giving most of it to the first charity on your list, the Nelson Campbell Foundation, which you personally control. Then approve just two more candidates – Abigail Cabot's School for Wayward Girls and whichever one of the remaining 14 charities offers you the best incentive to choose them.

Not to belabor the obvious, but choosing Abigail's School for Wayward Girls is a natural choice in that this will give you the opportunity to meet interesting people with whom you can do the hands-on work that is so dear to you.

Yes, Clarence, we are among those lucky people who feel the need to work amongst the dregs of humanity – for who will turn them around if we do not? In an attempt to identify the lowest of the low, I recently bought an issue of Hustler magazine in order to read Larry Flynt's list of hypocrites. Bob Barr was featured in that issue. He exemplifies the type of low-life who needs our help. As an aside, you might be shocked to learn that there are some rather lewd photos in this magazine. However, they can be ignored, or failing that, treated as pages in a coloring book.

For instance, I drew wings on some of the ladies, which made them look like the old masters' renderings of angels. As we both know, the human body is a vile and evil thing, and the hours I spent looking at them sickened me, but adding wings did soften the image. We do what we can.

But back to the purpose of my message. I want to welcome you, dear Clarence, to EJCF. I look forward to many happy and fulfilling days working with you as we tend our new flock. Surely, this is why we were put here on earth.

Your fellow fighter for good over evil,

Elton

Reverend Clarence Klotz

April 5, 1999

Dear Unc,

It's this man McDougall again. He seems fundamentally a good sort, but troubles follow him. A man with his credentials shouldn't need a confidence builder, but he does. This is where you come in. Do what you can. Your pay will be the same as last year.

If McDougall cannot be reached at his published address, try the police or his tennis club. Report to me when you have control of this delicate situation. Meanwhile, factor the following clues into your background file:

> There once was a senior from Mensa
> Who mixed his good works with nonsensa
> His humor contagious,
> His schemes were outrageous.
> At least all this was the consensa.

Ministerially,

Clarence

Uncle Randy
advisor to the wretched

April 7, 1999

Dear Clarence,

Thank you for your April 5 letter imploring me to help your friend, Gene McDougall. You might be surprised to learn that you are but one of many who have contacted me over the years about this unfortunate creature. As I understand it, you feel Mr. McDougall is lacking in self-confidence.

From what I know about him, just the opposite is true. His problem is <u>over</u>-confidence. How else do you explain why he has never requested a transfer from his A- league to a more appropriate B league? Everyone knows that he has the worst record of any member of his current A- league, yet he seems unable to accept the simple fact that he can no longer compete with A- players. He freely admits that he peaked athletically, intellectually and sexually in 1947 (and what a fine three months it was) and has been deteriorating ever since. Yet he tenaciously clings to the belief that he is just going through a long slump, and will soon come out of it.

In a way he is to be envied, not scorned. His fellow league members are the ones to be pitied, for it is they who must endure the indignity of spending 90 torturous minutes "playing tennis" with him every Saturday.

In short, Clarence, I believe the best thing we can do for Mr. McDougall is to leave him alone. Let us simply accept the bittersweet truth that he is quite happy living in a magic world all his own, sublimely unaware of his own ineptitude - not only as it applies to tennis but across the broad spectrum of life itself. Anyhow, I don't do pro bono work.

Regrettably,

R

Clarence Klotz
Beacon to the Lost, Friend to the Friendless, Oasis to the Weary

April 13, 1999

Dear Unc,

This is a last-ditch attempt to bring a lost but salvageable soul, your client Gene McDougall, out of the wilderness.

At 70 he is still active. This isolates him from 90 percent of his peers. Despite his downheartedness, he is still playing good tennis. This isolates him from 98 percent of his peers.

And even if he is not impressed by inclusion in the Chosen 2 Percent, consider that he is probably 20 years older than his average club opponent, hence deserving at least a theoretical handicap in observers' eyes. In addition,

1. He receives a lucrative pension and no longer has to work,
2. He gets discounts at restaurants and movie theaters,
3. He doesn't have to lift heavy boxes,
4. 50-year-olds call him "Sir,"
5. A teenage girl will occasionally give him her seat on the bus and
6. The bars of life are generally lowered.

Consider, too, that there's quite a talent difference between "A-" and "B." Your client would probably find "B" not challenging enough. But even if the opposite were true (which I doubt), who could blame a distinguished Super Senior from seeking greener pastures as the shadows lengthen? Many of the senior doubles participants are fugitives from singles leagues where life was becoming a little rough. Of course, doubles is a high price to pay for satisfaction. Perhaps the foregoing will help just a little.

Compassionately,

Clarence

Uncle Randy
advisor to the Wretched

April 23, 1999

Dear Clarence,

Your April 13 letter listing all the advantages Gene McDougall enjoys in life was a classic example of "the grass is always greener" syndrome. Actually, Mr. McDougall is barely able to keep his head above water as he frantically dog paddles his way through the cesspool of life. Let me comment on each of your well-meaning but inaccurate examples of his "privileged" status:

He receives a lucrative pension and no longer has to work.
True, but having to report to a loathsome dullard during his last 10 years in the corporate jungle caused him to suffer a heart attack and undergo bypass surgery. Money is nice, but at what price?

He gets discounts at restaurants and movie theatres.
This is true, but he is too sensitive to attend many movies because all too often he finds himself within earshot of women who visit with each other all through the show. Women are wonderful, social creatures, but as we all know, they belong in the kitchen or the bedroom. I'm sure you will agree that allowing them the vote and free access to such public places as movies is just plain wrong.

He doesn't have to lift heavy boxes.
Nobody has to do that. Sure, if your job requires such work, you will be fired, but hey - all actions have consequences.

50 year olds call him "sir."
Yes, strangers have occasionally addressed him in this manner, but people who know him tend to be much less deferential.

A teenage girl will occasionally give him her seat on the bus.
True, but this pales in comparison to what teenage girls were willing to do for him just a few short decades ago.

The bars of life are generally lowered.
Well, okay - maybe.

I hope this gives you a more realistic perspective - something you will need if you want to save this tortured soul. As a man of the cloth, this responsibility is yours - not mine. I am but a man. A splendid one to be sure, but still just a man.

Sadly,

Uncle Randy

Uncle Randy
advisor to the wretched

April 24, 1999

Dear Clarence,

I have had second thoughts about walking away from the challenge Gene McDougall represents. My high moral standards will not permit me to throw him to the wolves. It is just not right to give up on anyone, no matter how low he may be on the food chain.

I feel duty bound, therefore, to pass along some suggestions that might make him feel more at ease at the Hackers Haven Tennis Center, which, sadly, is where he spends most of his outside-the-house time.

- A membership cleansing policy should be put in place immediately. For starters, conduct an annual vote, with each club member casting one vote for the player he considers the biggest asshole in the club. Each year, the member garnering the most votes would have his sorry ass kicked out of the club. I understand that many years ago, when Mr. McDougall was gainfully employed, he made this suggestion at lunch one day, but did not push the idea further after one of his lunch companions asked him, "Would you abide by the vote?"

- Create more specific parameters for league participation. Skill levels have their place of course, but the club seems to be overlooking such possibilities as "The Bald-Headed League", "The Heart Bypass League" and "The Asshole League" (for those who qualify for that designation but have not yet won the annual "Biggest Asshole" vote). This would include the lowlifes who cheat, yell and scream at their opponents or lie about their age in order to enter age-specific tournaments. Hackers Haven could make a nice extra profit by selling tickets to watch the "Asshole League" matches, which would doubtless be much more hilarious than the Jerry Springer Show.

- And finally, as a gesture of respect for the elderly, permit men over 70 to join the women's leagues. This will give them a chance to win some matches, not to mention the opportunity to socialize afterwards as they share the hot tub and showers with their fellow league members.

Respectfully, *Uncle Randy*

Asshole League group picture.

Clarence Klotz
A light in the darkness, a haven to the weary

May 11, 1999

Dear Uncle,

It's an ill wind that blows nobody good (Shakespeare). Your man McDougall has blazed a long-needed trail to the study of assholes in America. Why hasn't anyone explored this so obviously fertile frontier before?

As with infant sciences, many basic questions need answering. Are assholes born or made? Do they possess an extra chromosome? Can they be cured? Do rating standards vary from nation to nation? Are there halfway houses for recovering assholes? Once an asshole, always an asshole? One recalls the overview of that unforgettable philosopher, George Eber, who estimated Hackers Haven Tennis Center's asshole presence at 1 to 2 percent, "compared with 10 percent in society generally."

Psychologists face the daunting reality that only 27.4 percent of America's assholes are aware that they are assholes. Thus the need for costly long-term one-on-one education. One envisions books or support groups with such titles as A Confederacy of Assholes, Twilight for Assholes and Assholes Anonymous (in which a jerk calls an alleged former jerk who attempts to talk the party of the first part out of proposed asshole activity). This could spark major research. You would receive a findings report shortly after any publication.

Mr. McDougall's proposal for the identification, treatment, segregation and expulsion of assholes at Hackers Haven Tennis Center has been taken under advisement and will be advanced to committee soon. While there is considerable anti-asshole sentiment in the membership ranks, security specialists among the employees are confident they will be able to handle any outbreaks of violence.

Your first letter of April 23 suggests a bevy of great book titles, to wit:

1 Dogpaddling Through the Cesspool of Life
2 What Price Money?
3 I Worked for a Loathsome Dullard
4 Keep 'em in the Kitchen and Bedroom

In the certain promise that McDougall can use just about any words to smile by, I offer some further nonsensa:

> There's an erudite senior from Mensa
> Devoid of a single pretensa.
> His spirits are low
> But shouldn't be so:
> His record needs no defensa.

Say not the struggle naught availeth (Arthur Clough, but isn't that a double negative?).

Exhortatively,

Clarence

Uncle Randy
advisor to the Wretched

May 15, 1999

Dear Clarence,

I was impressed by your scholarly and insightful May 11 letter regarding assholes. Your quoting such legends as Shakespeare, Clough and Eber certainly strengthened your already powerful message, and it surely did not hurt to throw in a few statistics and an inspirational original poem of your very own. Still, please permit me a few observations.

Regarding Eber's estimate that Hackers Haven is under-represented in assholes (1 or 2 percent versus the general population's 10 percent), the first figure can be verified anecdotally from my own experience. I personally know nine assholes at Hackers Haven. If I am correct in that the club has 900 members, this means those nine assholes represent 1 percent of the total – right in line with Eber's 1 to 2 percent assessment. However, his contention that assholes comprise about 10 percent of the earth's population is open to question, especially since the name, place, date and methodology of the underlying research was not specified. I believe that figure to be much higher than 10 percent.

This minor disagreement notwithstanding, I share your admiration and respect for George Eber. This, despite the fact that in the summer of '87, a few months after my heart bypass surgery, I beat him on clay 6-1, 6-0, eliciting his comment that, "If I had known you were going to do this to me, I would have gone to the hospital and pulled your plug."

But what I really want to address is your statement that 27.4 percent of America's assholes are not aware that they are assholes. Since this was stated as a fact and backed up by a percentage figure which included a decimal point, most people would have been overwhelmed and therefore blindly accepted your viewpoint as an indisputable fact. But I am made of sterner stuff. I believe the true figure is much closer to 100 percent. This, in spite of the fact that I know of at least one man (our mutual acquaintance, Gene McDougall) who has always made it a point to tell assholes that they are indeed assholes, and also taking the time to explain why. Sadly, however, he does not believe he has ever convinced any of them. Instead, many have taken umbrage at his remarks. Go figure.

Percentages aside, I'm sure we can all agree that there are more horses' asses than horses in this world. Although this is not good, everything has an upside. In this case, our knowledge of this situation will serve to keep us on the alert for road apples so we can kick them aside as we walk down the hazardous road of life.

Your big picture guy,

Uncle Randy

Uncle Randy
advisor to the Wretched

May 25, 1999

Dear Clarence,

A comment you made in your April 13 letter continues to trouble me. In reference to Gene McDougall, you mentioned that he was isolated from 90% of his peers because, at 70, he is still active.

This does not compute. If his being 70 is the reason for his isolation, what about when he was 50, 20, or 12? I have come to know him well enough so that I can speak to this issue with some authority. This is not an age-related problem. What the problem really is, or how to alleviate it, remains unclear.

Theories abound, but they remain just that – theories.

Would he have turned out differently if he had spent his youth in Coal City, Illinois instead of Baudette, Minnesota? Was it too cold in Baudette for children to develop normally? Were the local teachers in Baudette inferior to those in Coal City? After all, there are 3,901 people in bustling Coal City compared to 1,147 in relatively moribund Baudette. The lure of the big city all but guarantees that the best teachers would flock to Coal City, leaving Baudette to struggle along with the leftovers.

Also, with 3.4 times Baudette's population, Coal City is mathematically assured of spawning more historical heroes than Baudette. Two examples are William E. Sommerville, a world renowned expert on wire rope machine development in circa 1910, and more recently, Nelson Wellesley Campbell, noted author and tennis club magnate. Does Coal City's pride in these people create an atmosphere which encourages its young people to strive to live up to their rich heritage? This seems obvious, yet no scientific data have been gathered to substantiate any of this.

As a spiritual man, your duty is clear. Drink from the cup and do what you must to bring light where there has been only darkness. You can make a difference. I urge you to institute a scientific study. Compile Baudette and Coal City statistics so that we can uncover trends and compare murder rates, illegitimate births, speeding tickets, communist activity, wife-swapping, hangings (in effigy and for real), won-lost records of the high school basketball teams and all other measurable aspects of community life. There are lessons to be learned and exciting social advances to be enjoyed if we can uncover some actionable cause-and-effect relationships.

Godspeed,

Uncle Randy

Nelson Campbell

June 1, 1999

Dear Uncle,

How in blazes did you learn about Billy Sommerville? He was chronicled mostly as a regional aircraft pioneer. In the years just preceding World War I, he built Curtiss Jenny type planes and flew them from improvised fields. One of my late photographer sister's last projects was to restore some Sommerville plane photos and enlarge them for framed display in a local building.

While I was born in Coal City, I actually resided there only two years, one and a half after birth (at which point we followed coal to the southern Illinois fields) and six months after returning from the Navy. However, through visits, my parents who were natives, and my sister who lived and worked there for most of her career, I'm privy to most of whatever can pass for news in Coal City.

The major milestones in local history:

- The day in 1883 when 75 miners, a few of them only 13 or 14, were drowned when heavy rains flooded the shaft. (There were few safety regulations in those boom days, and the sinister suspicion persists that the ill-fated mine was the only one open that floody day.)

- The day circa 1909 when 11 local immigrants, seven Scots and four Italians, tied the Olympic and world's champion Glasgow soccer team on a field next to Miller's dance hall on Division Street. (En route to St. Louis after appearances in New York, Philadelphia and Pittsburgh, the Glasgow people must have wondered how a hamlet such as Coal City was slipped into the schedule. The score was 1-1.)

- The day circa 1965 when a field north of town was discovered to be the state's only stand of pristine vegetation, the way things were before even the Indians came. (Now known as Goose Lake Prairie with state status, its significance is downplayed by some local skeptics; "It's pristine only because them Collinses, who owned the land, were too shiftless to till it.")

In recent years Chicago sportswriters have had mild fun with the revelation that Coal City HS has been champion or at least a semifinalist several times in 3A or 2A state football playoffs. This would not be news very far outside Grundy County except that the school has sponsored the sport only since 1976. Before that "football" meant soccer in Coal City.

Today Coal City is a misnomer. There hasn't been a shaft mine in the area since circa 1930, and the last strip mine gave up the ghost in 1973. This was good coal (though high-sulfur), but the seam was thin. In the old days many of the miners built their homes on stilts. They knew they'd have to move down the road in a few years. Eventually there was no more "down the road." Meanwhile I grew up in a metropolis of 9,500, so you can see that we're dealing with a vastly different level of urbanity. We were even larger than International Falls. All this reminds an old wanderer of memorable sayings and lore surrounding small towns generally, to wit:

- "Always boost your home town, even though it be hell."

- "My home town is so small that redeeming soft-drink bottles is the No. 1 industry."

- "My home town is so small that when we go hunting, we go toward town."

- "The population of my home town is always the same. Every time a baby is born, some guy leaves town." (Herb Shriner)

The statistical research suggested in your letter of May 25 has been taken under advisement, and assignments have been made to the top minds in those fields. Governmental corruption (including speed traps) and fights following football and basketball games have been added to your quite comprehensive list of categories.

Now for the most important question of all. How did you learn that my middle name is Wellesley?! This has been a deliberately well-kept secret, the reasoning being that usage could encourage blackmail. You wouldn't consider that, would you?

Reverently,

Nelson

P.S. The "90 percent isolation" reference was in the context that only 10 percent of 70-year-olds - at best - could dream of playing tennis at the level of your man McDougall.

Uncle Randy

June 5, 1999

Dear Nelson,

You have expressed concern that I am in possession of some of your darkest secrets. And, of course, you are curious about how they came into my possession. Surely you must realize that I am duty-bound to protect my sources, but I can tell you this much. I have availed myself of the services of a man whose investigative techniques were honed to a fine edge during his years as an FBI agent, and perfected during his subsequent seven year project chronicling the life of a Soviet spy. This story will be available in book form in October. I'm sorry, but I cannot tell you any more without jeopardizing this man's cover. I know you will understand.

Rest easy about that middle name, my friend. I swear I will never divulge it to anyone. Believe me, I really do understand and sympathize. If my middle name were Wellesley, I would feel exactly as you do about keeping it under wraps. However, just in case you don't trust me and begin to flirt with the idea that silencing me would be your best way out, be forewarned that I have placed your middle name in an envelope and given it to someone who has instructions to turn it over to the police and the media if anything untoward should happen to me.

And finally, as a fellow aficionado of small town descriptions, permit me to add one more to your list – Larry Flynt's reply when asked about his formative early years, "I grew up in a part of Kentucky where the main industry was jury duty."

By the way, I also know that when you enrolled at the University of Illinois, your gave your address as Marion, Illinois. Isn't a federal prison located there? Just asking.

Respectfully,

R

Clarence Klotz

June 9, 1999

Dear Uncle Randy,

You are wise to withhold source information on Campbell/Coal City/Marion. We wouldn't want to expose the poor soul. The upshot is that you have at last been able to use the investigative reporting techniques learned at that bastion of journalism, the University of Minnesota. There will be other, similar challenges.

Add the following to our growing list of small-town characterizations:

- The ice cream "Flavor of the Week" in my home town was vanilla.

- One rural fellow's idea of real living as expressed in Ring Lardner's "Haircut": "Hod, if I had your money. I'd quit my job, move to the county seat, put up at the Hotel Mercer and see a different show every night."

- Marion *is* the nearest post office to the federal prison, but the distance from town is actually about seven miles. The facility is to be replaced by one in Colorado. Its inhabitants have included such worthies as John Gotti (still there). Pollard (who stole secrets for Israel) and the Puerto Rican nationalists who shot up the Senate. A minimum security prison is also part of the complex, and Pete Rose served his time there. This gave city sports writers a cute sidebar; Marion is the home town of Ray Fosse, the catcher with whom Rose had his celebrated home-plate collision in the all-star game.

Your "road apples" philosophy has so impressed me that I whipped up the doggerel below (this will teach you to philosophize):

> There's a venerable scholar from Mensa
> Who learning he's wont to dispensa.
> He knows about strife,
> The road apples of life,
> And that truth one cannot condensa.

Teddy sent me a dandy Donegal postcard from Ireland. She mentioned flying Aeroflot, for which she deserves a special prayer. Whatever its actual performance record, who needs professional PR more than Aeroflot?

Warmly,

Clarence

Thor Quixote
star-crossed crusader

June 20, 1999

Dear Ann Flanders,

The service sidewalk behind my townhouse is lower than the ground in my back yard. The same is true of my neighbor's back yard. (Her townhouse is behind mine on the other side of the sidewalk.) As a result, the water and mud from both yards drains down onto the sidewalk where it remains as an eyesore and a physical danger most of the time. In the winter, it is solid ice. This problem, which I have been complaining about for years, will finally be addressed this summer.

One would think the solution would be to raise the ten feet of sidewalk that is lower than the adjacent lawns. But as it was explained to me, they plan to dig a trench alongside the entire 50 yards of sidewalk, lay drainage pipes to the main drainage area and then put a drainage grate in the ground next to the sidewalk. This means the drainage grates will be higher than the sidewalk As I see it, this could work only in the unlikely event that the water would run uphill.

This whole thing has pushed me one step closer to full-blown agoraphobia. I feel safe in the house as long as I don't answer the phone or attempt to fix any electrical or mechanical devices.

But I digress. My question is this: Should I (a) attempt to be an agent of change and finally accede to the wishes of those who have urged me to become a board member, (b) chuck it all and move to a tropical paradise such as Hawaii, Tahiti or Guam or (c) make a statement by arming myself to the teeth, attending the next board meeting and taking out as many of them as I can?

Despondently,

Thor

Marcus Aurelius
Abraham Lincoln Smith
Counselor of last resort

July 2, 1999

Dear Mr. Quixote,

Ann Flanders has given me your challenging, provocative, perplexing, disturbing letter of June 20.

This is but an introductory letter, a mere overview of a case possibly demanding a series of face-to-face consultations. For the moment I would ask only that you heed the wisdom of the ancient Hindu ascetic Rhanga Vitta:

"A man has not fulfilled his destiny nor justified his brief time on earth nor made peace with himself until he has, just once, stood firm against the establishment and in the process done the right, most intelligent thing."

I have two other recommendations. First, don't retire to Guam under any circumstances. and second, don't resort to violence. Even if "dream team" attorneys get you off, you'll still have to sneak around alleys. Meanwhile I am enclosing a work by another distinguished citizen, Dave Barry, who is pondering entry into public service.

Cordially,

Marc

Reverend Elton Jones

July 10, 1999

Dear Marcus,

My good friend, Thor Quixote, sent me your reply to his plea to Ann Flanders for help. While he was disappointed to see that the reply came not from Ann but from you, a complete stranger, he did appreciate the irony of his unwilling involvement in what can only be described as a paper version of the voice mail runaround so familiar to all of us these days. He has decided to solve this as well as most of his other problems by staying home more and limiting contact with the outside world. That is why he asked me to answer your letter for him. The poor soul has simply lost interest in continuing his life-long losing battle against God, Nature, and City Hall.

And anyhow, that whole (hole?) drainage problem turned out to have been nothing more than an unfortunate failure to communicate. As it turns out, the 50 feet of drainage pipe already existed underground. What they did was grade the adjacent lawn lower than the low part of the sidewalk, dig a hole at that spot, hook into the underground drainage pipe and cover the hole with a grate. Since these plans were never made known to the membership, rumors rushed in to fill the void.

Thor also sent me your enclosure, an article by Dave Barry. Excellent! Dave now has a new fan. I would vote for him. God, how I wish our politicians consisted solely of such people as Dave Barry, Barney Frank, Larry Flynt and Jesse Ventura! These four epitomize all that I hold dear – humor, intelligence, courage, a loathing of hypocrites and a commitment to hold the people's interests above those of the special interest groups who have made whores out of 98% of our "representatives" in Congress. I would have called them prostitutes, but prostitutes deliver what they promise - a noble trait which, alas, is notably lacking in Congress.

It is this unprincipled behavior by our elected officials that contributes to flag-burnings. So, in a classic example of curing the symptom while ignoring the disease, the politicians pander to the most ignorant among us by mindlessly attempting to add an amendment to our constitution banning the burning of our flag. I assume this means the next time our flag is burned in some place such as Iran, we will send paratroopers to ferret out the perpetrators and bring them to justice.

On the other hand, maybe I am just a grouch. Your perspective is highly valued and earnestly solicited.

Introspectively,

Elton

Reverend Clarence Klotz

July 14, 1999

Dear Elton,

Your recent comments to Marcus Smith were right on the money. Given the problems of the United States of America, what more sophomoric expression of detachment and/or pandering to the not-so-bright right than to man a crusade against flag burning?

We have a national gun problem that no nation ever had, yet we can solve it by posting the Ten Commandments on bulletin boards and in locker roams? That's like thinking we can abolish war on earth by simply sending copies of the Golden Rule to every head of state.

As to prostitution in government, consider that 75 to 80 percent of the American people want tougher gun legislation, yet 51 percent has been a virtual impossibility in Congress. It's on public record that the NRA pays from $10,000 to $100,000 a year to its favorites or potential favorites in Congress; who would want to blow that, even if it means risking a loss at the polls? It doesn't take a PhD to see a correlation between contributions and votes.

Try the following as commentary on the flag situation:

> This don't-burn-the-flag legislation?
> Mere ploy of the crassly despotic
> For hoodwinking gullible voters
> Who'll perceive them as "more patriotic,"
> And how would you handle the wording?
> As soldiers and Boy Scouts have learned,
> A flag that is torn or unsightly
> Is always, per protocol, burned.

Keep the faith, brother,

Clarence

Reverend Elton Jones, CEO
Elton Jones Rehabilitation Center

July 19, 1999

Dear Clarence,

As a patriotic American, you have been selected to become an honorary board member of the newly formed Elton Jones Rehabilitation Center. As such, you will be expected to assist the Center in its efforts to help a fellow American, Good Conduct Medal winner Gene McDougall, who served nobly in our armed forces during the Korean Conflict and is still paying a terrible price for those years of suffering and torment. True, he was not in a war zone, but he constantly worried that he could be sent to one. He was torn between actually wanting that to happen or staying on Guam, where women were rarer than an honest politician. Keep in mind that he was there for 28 wretched months. Spending much of his early twenties living this unnatural life of near-celibacy has left scars that he bears to this day. In a word (seven words, actually), he cannot form successful relationships with women.

Each sexual encounter he could have had if he had been anywhere but Guam, multiplied by the average weight of each woman who would have been involved, puts him about 55 tons behind the curve. Since then, in a frantic effort to recoup this lost tonnage, he has rushed into unwise relationships, resulting in a sorry history of failed romances. After 25 years of marriage, his wife decided that enough was enough and moved 2,000 miles away from him to live in Arizona. After that, he found another woman willing to live with him, but after 10 years of that, she also moved out. Not just out of his house, not just out of the city, not just out of the state, but out of the country – far, far out of the country to one of the least appealing places on earth – Russia. I'm sure you would agree that such a drastic step speaks volumes.

Donations will be gratefully accepted and receipts furnished. Whether those receipts can be used to lower your taxes is something you will need to discuss with your accountant. But money is not the only way you can help. Please check around and see whether you can find any nurturing, caring women (preferably young and beautiful who don't mind being mistreated) who would like to meet this man. He has gray hair with a wide part in the middle (about 11 inches), a scraggly beard, a high-pitched, rather annoying voice and a bent-over, wrinkled, frail 70-year-old body. However, within that admittedly less than inspiring exterior dwells a much younger person (a nine-year-old boy).

It is said that there is someone out there for each of us. Although we may be dealing here with an exception to the rule, let us not give up without a struggle. Please help.

God bless you,

Elton

Clarence Klotz

July 21, 1999

Dear Elton,

I am pleased beyond words to be associated with EJRC. Expecting the undersigned to be of romantic assistance to anyone is like expecting Dizzy Dean to teach English or Leon Spinks to teach driver ed, but what loyal American would run from a challenge?

This old warrior finds some parallel in a Harry Caray talk-show interview of some years ago:

CALLER: Harry, you were in St. Louis for 25 years. Why did you leave?
CARAY: Well, there was a rumor that I was having an affair with Mrs. Busch. It wasn't true, but I was so flattered that I let it ride and took the consequences.

So even the remotest connection with romance flatters me. I will help EJRC in any way possible except that I will not do any telemarketing or door-to-door fund raising. Please understand that you are dealing with an elder who cherishes these bromides and passages:

- Don't buy any green bananas.
- Accept the facts that type is not getting smaller, stair steps are not getting higher and the distance from the baseline to the net is not getting longer.
- Keep maladies to yourself; the only thing worse than arthritis is listening to someone tell you about it.
- Look on age as a lusty winter, frosty but kindly.
- Picture old age as "serene and bright, as lovely as a Lapland night" (Perhaps more applicable to Minnesota).
- If you don't have a plan, stay in the car.

Good hunting, brother,

Clarence

Reverend Elton Jones

August 10, 1999

Dear Clarence,

As a socially responsible citizen, I believe it is incumbent upon me to address the latest issue of public concern. Accordingly, I have devised a plan to significantly reduce the anger and hatred exemplified by the recent school shootings in our country.

I read somewhere that there is a special combination of chromosomes in most violent criminals. I can't remember where I read it or what the combination was, but as a big picture man, I will brush the minutia aside and get right to the point.

It seems clear to me that we should determine the chromosomes of each person in the country and humanely execute all those whose chromosomes identify them as potential killers. This need only be done once if a program were simultaneously implemented requiring that, from that point forward, all newborns would be subjected to this same chromosome check, with all that group's potential criminals being put to death on the spot. Of course, foreigners entering our country would also be examined and either deported or released into our general population as appropriate. If this plan had been in effect during the entire century now drawing to a close, we would never have had to deal with such people as Hitler, Sadaam Hussain (you spell it – I can't be bothered) and Milosovic.

A side-benefit might be the eradication of those slimy bastards who engage in audio-violence by hanging wind chimes in their yards to bedevil their neighbors day and night without end.

I do not know my own chromosome combination, but I do know that I abhor violence. Therefore, if my chromosome exam places me in the violence-prone group, that theory is invalidated, leaving global warming as the only logical cause of the problem (since crime increases as temperatures rise). I dare say that a comparison of crime rates in Antarctica versus Miami will bear this out. I would provide the statistics, but they will be more meaningful to you if you do the research yourself. Besides, I am old and weary of pissing on the electric fence of life decade after decade – always with the same unpleasant results.

Yours for a better world, *Elton*

Chromosome impaired churchgoers at a Sunday social.

Clarence Klotz

Friday the 13th August, 1999

Dear Colleague Elton,

You make me think too much. Certainly your "criminal chromosomes" plan would eventually relieve school overcrowding, reduce highway congestion and give more business to morticians, thus boosting the national GNP. If we liquidated a few potential Lincolns or Einsteins in the process, who would ever know? We'd feel good about ourselves, and isn't that the most important thing?

I have a corollary plan for those convicted of major hate crimes: shoot them in the legs and let them lie and die in the street without medical attention. They're bullies (and generally losers contributing nil to society), so let them be on the receiving end for a change. If we execute them with customary fanfare, they become martyrs. If we give them prison without parole, they cost taxpayers more per annum than a Harvard education. In the slammer they'd probably infect others, thus we'd be aggravating the problem. Good riddance!

Now for an educational program; explain to John Q. Citizen that the NRA is simply a trade association formed to promote the sale of guns, not a society of God-fearing constitutionalists at a town meeting. There's nothing wrong with being a legitimate trade association; it's just that people should be made to realize that the NRA is no more than that.

As for the Second Amendment argument, give me a break. Those apparently hallowed words were inserted into the Bill of Rights at a time when we didn't yet have a standing army or National Guard. Only militias. And for all their wonderful contributions and selfless devotion, the framers of the Constitution weren't perfect. Benjamin Franklin had more things going in

Washington, Philadelphia and Paris than Kennedy, Harding and Clinton ever dreamed of, and the boys signed an "all men are created equal" covenant while owning slaves. Was it Jefferson who said that when community and individual rights are in conflict, community always wins?

Issues to think on, brother.

Collegially,

Clarence

Reverend Elton Jones
spiritual guru and entrepreneur

September 17, 1999

Dear Clarence,

Eureka!

Yesterday, while standing in a long, slow moving line at the post office to buy a stamp, an idea was born which I believe will become the next franchising sensation to sweep the country - a lawn chair rental service just outside every post office in this great country of ours. At last, postal patrons need no longer to stand in long lines. They can SIT in line. I have patented this idea and am currently licensing franchisees for a fee of just $1,000 per post office per year. This is a moneymaker. The $1,000 annual fee multiplied by the tens of thousands of post offices in the USA amounts to many millions of dollars for our (well okay, my) coffers each year. But I have not forgotten about you. No, indeed. At $1.00 per chair, you could make at least $100 a day - and you could double that by simply raising your rental fee to $2.00. A TIP FOR YOU: Make it $1.99. Since 98% of people are dumber than average, they will think $1.99 is just over $1.00 and they will beat a path to your door.

As you know, this is not my first get-rich-quick scheme. I have decided to make my entire treasury of business ideas available via franchises. This includes my popular Door-to-Door Breast Exam Service (Service With a Smile)* as well as my Mom and Pop Fire Stations (start small with a used Ford Pinto and a fire extinguisher, and build up to your own fleet of big red trucks, dalmatians and all.) Literature describing these business opportunities was sent to you previously, as was my one-man-band idea (specializing in funerals, weddings and basketball games). This one has so far failed to get off the ground (too far ahead of its time) but has enormous potential. I am making all these winners available on a first come, first served basis. Why? Simply because life has been so good to me that I feel compelled to give a little something back. Franchising these "no-brainer" moneymakers is my way of saying "thank you."

Yours for a life of wealth and privilege,

Elton

* The original Door to Door Breast Exam Service was predicated on a $10 payment per exam. That franchise is still available, but I now have a sister franchise called The <u>Complimentary</u> Door to Door Breast Exam Service. This is the same as the original except that, upon completion of the exam, the salesman pays the client an appropriate compliment instead of $10. This helps the bottom line immensely by bringing cash flow out of the red all the way to the break-even point (before expenses). An experienced operator can also expect quite a few tips and favors of one kind or another - a type of remuneration which often falls through the cracks, IRS reporting-wise (if you know what I mean).

Reverend Clarence Klotz
Friend to the Friendless

September 28, 1999

Dear Brother Elton

You've done it again! First, the door-to-door breast exam service. Then the mom 'n pop fire station. And now a lawn chair rental service for post office patrons. Thanks for letting me in on the ground floors.

As one who lists a rubber ruler that stretches or contracts (as objectives may be) and a vacuum pipe system for routing junk mail directly from box to incinerator among his contributions to capitalism, I appreciate creativity wherever it surfaces.

Why not extend your lawn chair idea to banks, which are less subject to regulations governing federal structures and at least on occasion have just as much need for your service? A few years ago I waited interminably in a long line at Mt. Prospect's Countryside Bank (successively NBD, First Chicago, and Bank One. Maybe next year Bank Two)? Not armed with a tape recorder, I lost some of the better consumer comments, but the following remain:

- "I've been in line so long I'll have to change the date on my check for cash, and I've missed two meals."

- "I know now why there are so many bank robberies. The lines are so long that's the only way patrons can get any money."

- "If anybody asks me to recommend a neighborhood that needs another bank, guess what I'll tell him."

Hang in there, brother. It's creativity, rather than words or guns, that moves civilization. Jonathan Swift said, "A nice man is a man of nasty ideas." Ponder that one. Given our personalities, might the converse be true - that nasty men brook nice ideas?

How many lawn chairs in your first order?

Affectionately,

Clarence

Reverend Elton Jones
spiritual icon and start-up business wizard

September 30, 1999

Dear Clarence,

I know you are still reeling from the cornucopia of business franchises I recently made available to you. Well, hang on to your hat, because I have some more opportunities for sale - and I'm letting each of them go for only $100 or best offer. In all honesty, these bargain prices are the result of my having tried all these seminars which, for one reason or another, did not fly. However, an innovative man such as yourself could make a few changes and possibly hit it big with one or more of them. Perhaps getting a celebrity such as Dan Rostenkowski or Henry Hyde to be your guest speaker is all it would take. I understand both of these people have been recent guest speakers at Loyola University – at the behest of Loyola's Center for Ethics. (Yes, the Center for Ethics. Trust me – this is not a typo.) Anyhow, here are the seminar titles:

- Group Sex as a Networking Tool
- Voice Mail Rage Management
- Lying and Cheating for Fun and Profit
- Recluse Party Guide
- So You Want to be a Prostitute
- Shoplifting as a Career
- Do It Yourself Vasectomies
- Sell Your Soul and be in Congress

As you can see, each of these titles is a powerful attention grabber. People will not be able to ignore them any more than they could drive by an auto accident without gaping. Managed properly, these seminars are money in the bank. It's your move.

Carpe diem,

Elton

Reverend Elton Jones

October 1, 1999

Dear Clarence,

As benevolent men of the cloth, I believe we should cut Henry Hyde some slack. He did not invent hypocrisy. He merely brought it to a new level. After all, it is man's nature, a sad truth I discovered in my early teenage years.

Although this was a long time ago, I still vividly remember taking a short cut through the neighbor's back yard one night while walking home, and noticing a light in the window. The shade had been pulled down, but not quite all the way. Being a curious young fellow, I got a little closer and looked in. Lo and behold, there was the neighbor's comely teenage daughter undressing for bed. I was so thrilled that when I saw my friends the next day I told them all about it, whereupon they admonished me for being a Peeping Tom.

Now comes the ironic part of the story. At about the same time the next night, as I again stood peering into the window, I heard a twig snap. Someone was only a few feet away and approaching me from around the corner. It was too late to turn and run, so I just stood there. To my great relief, it turned out to be my friend Fred, who had been my most vocal critic earlier in the day. We watched the show together, and a good time was had by all.

This demonstration of hypocrisy undoubtedly provided a good many lessons to be learned, but they elude me. Perhaps you, a man whose fertile brain conceived the rubber ruler and the junk mail vacuum pipe system, could enlighten me.

Please advise,

Elton

The venerable reverend Elton Jones

November 27, 1999

Dear Clarence,

It is lamentable that tending our flocks has kept us so busy lately that we have not found time to keep in touch. With so much misery and chicanery to overcome, it becomes even more important that we share our experiences and insights, the better to accomplish our glorious mission here on earth.

The latest abomination to come to my attention is the anonymous spreading of rumors that Senator McCain is too unstable to be President because of his five and a half years as a prisoner in Viet Nam. Obviously, these are the same people who, a year or two ago, circulated a list of Clinton acquaintances who had died violently – the implication being that he had something to do with those deaths. Despicable! By my senior year in high school, at least a dozen of my friends and acquaintances had committed suicide, drowned or been killed in train, plane and car accidents.

Such malicious hate-mongers are destined to spend eternity in Hell. It is our job to save them, and yet I must confess that I am sometimes tempted to abandon them to their fate.

I am turning to you for the faith and strength I need to carry on. I know you will not fail me.

Plaintively,

Elton

Clarence Klotz

November 30, 1999

Dear Elton,

As I extricate myself from pesky tasks and prepare to consume your current missives, I pause to react briefly but most positively to yours of November 27th:

"Those who supported Richard Nixon twice are worried about McCain's alleged instability?"

My favorite political cartoon of the moment is headed "Foreign Affairs Résumé." It has two panels. The left panel, showing a map of Southeast Asia, bears the caption below "McCain: 5 1/2 years." The right panel, showing an International House of Pancakes restaurant, bears the caption "Bush: 45 minutes."

What does it say about the electorate in the world's greatest and most sophisticated country that political managers can avoid burning issues and deal essentially in personalities and innuendo? As for The Shrub (as columnist Molly Ivins calls young Bush), he must be causing his moneyed supporters some sleepless nights. You can be a governor of a state without taking a stand on anything, but a candidate for President?

Collegially,

Clarence